DOMESTIC VIOLENCE IN THE HEADLINES

None of these women thought it would happen to them!

The Tacoma police chief met his estranged wife in a parking lot to pick up their children, ages 5 and 8, for scheduled visitation. After placing the children in the back seat of his car, the chief returned to his wife's car, got into the front seat, and shot her in the head. He then shot himself. Witnesses said the two children ran to their mother's side when she attempted to crawl out of the car.
Source: Associated Press

A 48-year-old Eatontown man murdered his wife by stabbing her and slitting her throat with a butcher knife. He then took his own life. Authorities said the couple was in the throes of divorce.
Source: GMNews.com

A 38-year-old mother of five's fight with domestic abuse ended tragically this morning when her estranged husband fatally shot her in the head in front of her home, and then shot himself. The children were present in the home at the time of the shooting.
Source: The Garden City Telegram

Authorities say a man who was being treated for mental problems fatally shot his wife and their daughter on Christmas day, and he then killed himself. The victims were identified as Nicole Young, believed to be in her late 20s, and her 14-month-old daughter, Haley. The couple was in the process of a divorce.
Source: The Associated Press

Police believe Mark Allen Ebert, 37, shot his wife Lisa Lynn Ebert, 35, twice and himself once with a 12-gauge shotgun. Lisa Ebert had previously obtained a restraining order against her husband. In a deadly six-week stretch in June and July, four women -- all military wives -- were murdered in that region.
Source: MSNBC News

The Emergency Divorce Handbook for Women

Angela Hoy

ISBN 1-59113-324-6

THE EMERGENCY DIVORCE HANDBOOK FOR WOMEN

Copyright © 2003 by Angela Hoy

Published by Booklocker.com, Inc. – http://www.booklocker.com

Booklocker.com books may be purchased for business or promotional use or for special sales. For information, please contact:
Booklocker.com, Inc.
P.O. Box 2399
Bangor, ME 04402
Email: richard@booklocker.com

Booklocker.com, Inc. - 2003

Printed in the United States of America.

DISCLAIMER

This book is not a legal resource. You must obtain legal advice when separating or getting a divorce. The author, contributors, and publisher are not responsible for any actions or outcomes resulting from reading this book. Get legal advice, protect yourself, and don't act until you have a plan in place.

Warning. If your partner/spouse finds this book before you announce your intent to separate or divorce, you may be in danger. If your relationship is already troubled, your spouse may already be going through your things. Also, your partner may read this book to determine what actions you are contemplating. Please, if you are reading this book and are fearful for your physical, emotional and/or financial safety, hide it in a safe place.

With Gratitude

This book would not have been possible without the contributions from the brave women who've shared their stories herein. I'm honored and blessed to have my writing appear alongside theirs.

To my children. Everything I do is for you. Since I first held each of you in my arms, your love and smiles are what have made my life worth living.

To my husband, Richard Hoy, my reluctant hero. He doesn't think he's done anything heroic, but, as you'll read in these pages, he has, in abundance. There just aren't many men in the world like Richard Hoy. Thanks also to his parents, Cindy and Dale, for raising such an incredibly loving and selfless man. And thanks to all the Hoys and Blums, including Granny Rita (gotcha!), Grandma (Irma) Hoy, Becky Litwin, and Grandpa (Bill) and Grandma (Thelma) Blum for welcoming my children with love and for making them feel like they've been part of your family forever.

To my mom, dad, sister, and brothers, who held my hand and supported my breaking heart throughout my marriage and divorce.

Additional and sincere thanks and hugs go out to the following wonderful people for their support: Sylvia Pond, LCSW, David Spang, MSW, LCSW, Anne Hanlon, MD and Corey Webb, PA-C (thank you all for helping our children through their grief!); my dear friend Melisse Shapiro; my step-daddy Leroy Manka (thanks for taking care of Mom!), Cathi Stevenson, and Jane S.E. Clayton, Esq. and Edward C. Spaight, Esq. (the best and most compassionate legal team in New England).

To "Jane" (see page xi for her story), who has left town without a trace. May God keep you and your boys safe and may you find the happiness and peace you so desperately deserve.

And, finally, blessings to the unknown man mentioned on page 8, whom I will never be able to thank in person.

Table of Contents

Introduction

When I first considered getting a divorce, I had no money and no access to legal advice. I was absolutely clueless as to what my first step should be. Only after my divorce was final did I look back and finally understand the process.

During my 12½-year marriage, I often thought about divorce. However, I was afraid – afraid of being alone, afraid of being broke, and afraid of the psychological impact divorce would have on my children. I never, ever thought that a divorce would result in my husband turning unpredictable with rage. He had always been emotional, but not a violent person. Had I known what would happen when the separation was taking place, I'd have made definite plans and done things a lot differently.

Many people came to my aid during my divorce, but only after I asked for help. This book is my way of giving back some of what I received - inspiration, unsolicited advice, and courage. The women's stories appearing here will help explain the emotional and frightening aspects of the divorce process that you won't find in other books, while also inspiring you to take the next steps to your new life of happiness. The stories appearing here share the things that each woman wishes she'd known before her marriage deteriorated.

One day last year, the mother of my son's best friend (I'll call her Jane) called me to ask for advice. She was trying to apply for a protective order against her husband and did not have an attorney. She knew I'd obtained one against my ex-husband. I readily agreed, wanting to help in any way I could. I also offered to drive her to the courthouse, the local women's shelter, and to help her apply for food stamps and welfare.

On that day, while we were at the social service office, Jane's mother was watching her two sons. She called Jane's cell phone to warn that the husband had just phoned and threatened to pick up the sons. I advised Jane to call her mother back and tell her to leave immediately with the boys. Her mother did so and, while she was driving away, passed the husband on the road. He turned around and followed them to a stoplight, where he jumped out of his car. Jane's mother hit the accelerator as the husband opened the back door and dragged their oldest son out of the car…out of the *moving car*!

If your spouse is screaming at you when you're together, brainwashing your children, hiding money from you, halting your access to finances, trying to make you lose your job, harming you or the children physically, or even just doing subtle, bizarre things that make you nervous, you must act to protect yourself and your children <u>now</u>.

Your spouse may be experiencing Divorce Psychosis, which can render his behavior unpredictable, intense, and even deadly. Do NOT assume that this non-violent person who you've known for years will not do something extreme. Refer back to the very first page of this book. The dead women mentioned there never would have believed their husbands capable of murder.

Divorce Psychosis is a term used increasingly by law enforcement and mental health professionals. It describes the emotional instability that often affects people who are going through a separation or divorce. Divorce Psychosis can result in physical and psychological abuse and even death, affecting the spouse, the children, and occasionally extended family members as well.

A woman can't predict what her husband will do when she starts separation or divorce proceedings. I recommend you assume the worst-case scenario.

This book is <u>not</u> a legal handbook. It is an emotional survival handbook. Women here have shared their stories, hoping you will learn from them and avoid making the same mistakes they did. And they want you to gain strength from their experiences.

This book uses the terms "spouse" and "husband" liberally. Either term may also apply to your "partner" whether you're married or not. Child custody and financial issues are battled in court regardless of the marital status of a couple.

Most of the names have been changed to protect the women and children involved.

Where to Get Help <u>Today</u>!

What you need right now:
Food, clothing, shelter, money, and protection

You won't find listings for women's shelters in the phone book. Often, these shelters are group homes located inconspicuously in neighborhoods. The homes must be anonymous in order to protect the women they're housing from abusive partners. In aiding Jane last year, I discovered that one women's shelter was only ½ mile from my home, located in a beautiful Victorian house. I'd have never known it was a women's shelter if I hadn't visited it myself.

Similarly, there are many resources available to women in need that are not public knowledge. You need only ask for help to have access to these services.

Do not hesitate to ask for immediate help if you need it! Your local women's shelter can put you in a safe place <u>tonight</u>. Even if you're not certain you're in danger, you can call them and talk to an understanding woman who will do everything she can to help you. They can even offer advice for navigating the courts and will have resources available to help you find free legal aid if you qualify.

Don't assume you are alone in your pursuit of safety, and affordable or free aid. There is help out there. You just need to know who to call. To find help in your area, call:

National Domestic Violence Hotline
1-800-656-HOPE

1-800-787-3224 (TDD)
Telecommunication Device for the Deaf

A large list of resources by state is available online at:
http://www.feminist.org/911/crisis.html

What to say when you call:
"I need to leave my husband and I don't know what to do."

They'll take it from there.

Should You Get Divorced?

This book is intended to assist women with the emotional issues that are involved with separation, divorce and child custody. This book is not intended to persuade women to leave their spouses or partners

You will recognize a great deal of anger and resentment in the women's stories in this book. These women have survived pain that some of us can't even imagine. It takes a long time to get over losing your children, your home, your job, and, in some cases your mind, at the hands of someone you used to love.

While it may appear some of us are bashing men, we openly recognize there are good men in the world. Most of us are now remarried to wonderful men!

So, should you get divorced or not? Only you know the answer to that question.

Where do you picture yourself a year from now? What do you want your life to be like? Can you imagine yourself living the next 1, 5 or 10 years with your current spouse? If so, and you're reading this book, you should contact a marriage counselor. If not, perhaps it's time to take action. If you are living with an alcoholic or drug addict, things aren't likely to get better. With addictions, life will probably continue to get worse. Ask any alcohol or drug counselor and they'll agree.

My ex-husband (I'll call him Eugene) was not physically abusive. He only harmed me physically once (he tried to throw me after pouring beer on my computer keyboard). But, he was very emotional and highly volatile. I never knew what would spark his temper. He would get drunk or smoke marijuana (he did other drugs, too, but not as frequently) and then go from crying to yelling to laughing and back again. And then, in an instant, or sometimes the next morning, he would be loving and apologetic. I never knew what mood he would be in at night and I did not completely know the damage his irregular actions and emotions were doing to our children. I thought that, with calculated words and actions, I could control his mood swings. I thought I was capable of changing him.

No one ever told me 'you can't change an alcoholic'. I wish they had. Only an alcoholic can change him or herself. I spent 12½ years desperately trying to mold my husband into somebody that he would never be.

I knew, before I even got married, that Eugene was an alcoholic. But, I was pregnant. I would never give up my baby, so I felt I had no other option but to get married. To marry in my church, we were required to go to pre-marital counseling with my minister. When we met with him, I told the minister Eugene had a drinking problem. The minister immediately pulled out a piece of paper, wrote down the name of a therapist, and said he was not qualified to deal with alcoholism. He then sent us on our way and didn't require any further pre-marital counseling. And, he married us. To this day, I feel this man did us a grave injustice. We, of course, never called that therapist. Young couples with a baby on the way can't afford therapists.

Your Current Life: The Big Picture

In a manipulative, abusive relationship, life usually descends from bliss to hell over a period of several years. Often, after the relationship ends, the victim will look back at her life, at the big picture, and think, "Oh my God. How did my life get that bad? Why didn't I notice it sooner?"

On a sunny day in March, when I was 19, I was 3 months pregnant and walking down the aisle with a handsome young man. If you'd pulled me aside at that moment and told me that, in a dozen years, I'd be cleaning his urine off the floor at night, scrambling to pay the bills alone because my husband couldn't keep a job, facing mounting debt because of excessive spending on beer and marijuana, and frequently finding hidden drug paraphernalia in my home, I'd have gone running and screaming out the chapel door.

Only after I'd lived with an alcoholic and had him removed from the home, and only after I started to live a "normal" life, did I look back and realize the disgusting and self-deprecating life I'd been living. It didn't all happen overnight. But, in the end, it was all happening simultaneously. I'd become so accustomed to all the pieces that make up an alcoholic's wife's existence that I could no longer recognize the horrors in my life.

Today, make a list of the most troublesome things about your life. If someone had handed you a list like that on your wedding day, and said, "This will be your life someday," what would you have done? What are you going to do about it now?

My Final Decision

Only a few months after our marriage, Eugene came home one night, drunk, and passed out on the bed. While undressing him, I found blood on his underwear. The next morning, he tried to tell me that a woman had sat on his lap in the bar, but that he'd pushed her off. I didn't believe him because the blood wasn't on his pants, only his underwear. I was absolutely devastated. Already pregnant and emotionally vulnerable, I never did get over that hurt or the resulting distrust. Years later, Eugene admitted to me that he'd "fooled around" with a woman he'd met at the bar that night.

A year or so after that incident, when the marriage had already begun to sour, I was lonely and sought the companionship of our next-door-neighbor, who was also in a bad marriage (and also an alcoholic). When things got physical, I instantly stopped the relationship. I then spent weeks with chronic stomach problems because I was experiencing so much guilt. A few years later, the exact same thing happened with an old high school friend. Once things got physical, I ran and was, again, sick with guilt, though not as severely as the previous time. I regret those mistakes, but I also understand that I was an insecure young woman desperate for someone to love me more than alcohol and drugs.

As the years passed, I grew hardened by my situation and I no longer loved or even liked Eugene. His touch disgusted me and I cringed whenever he walked in the door, not knowing if he'd be drunk, sober, happy or angry. But, I was determined to stay together "for the children."

After I'd been married for about 8 years, I hit bottom. Things had gotten so bad that I was thinking about suicide. Yet, even while thinking about it, I knew I'd never kill myself and leave my children alone. My thoughts scared me so badly that I made an appointment with my doctor. Once there, I nervously admitted, "I've been thinking about suicide. But, of course, I'd never do it because I have three children."

He replied, in a matter of fact tone, "Women with children kill themselves everyday."

He put me on anti-depressives. I suffered from clinical depression for four more years. The month my divorce was finalized was the month the doctor weaned me from the medication. I've been

4

depression-free ever since. That medication probably saved my life. I know it saved my sanity.

After 10 years of marriage, I finally gave up. However, I did not want to be alone. While I now regret this (because it further proves my weakness of fearing being alone), I actively and consciously sought a replacement for Eugene while still married. I finally found him, a man I met online who lived in Australia. Years later, I realized this would have never worked out. But, the blessing in my bad judgment was that Eugene found out about my online "affair." He promised to stop drinking if I would stay with him. He visited our doctor (the same one who'd put me on anti-depressives), started going to Alcoholics Anonymous (AA), and became a vocal supporter of the program.

For the next two years, our marriage was stable and happy, happier than it had ever been. Then, he abruptly stopped going to his AA meetings. At that time, he said he realized he "had never been an alcoholic", that he had just been irresponsible.

In December of that year, he started to secretly drink again. When I realized he was getting drunk and possibly doing drugs (he was very bad at hiding marijuana in the house – I found it everywhere), I gave up. I remember my shoulders slumping when I realized he'd came home drunk that night, after two years of sobriety. I didn't even need to reconsider my instant realization and decision. He was never going to stop drinking. Things would never get better. They would continue to get worse and there was nothing at all that I, nor my children, nor anybody else could do to make him stop. It was over. I was going to get a divorce.

So, what did I do then? Did I call a lawyer? No. Again, I set out to find Eugene's replacement. I was, again, afraid of being alone.

My father died when I was five years old. Even though my mom remarried quickly and her new husband adopted my brother and me, I've realized, over the years, that I suffer from an abandonment mentality. As soon as I was old enough to have a boyfriend, I got one. I continued to have a stream of boyfriends throughout my life, jumping from one to the next. If I felt the need to drop one, I'd find a replacement first. That is how badly I feared being alone, not having a boy (and later a man) to lean on.

So, I found Eugene's replacement. Though I had no plans to remarry, at least I had someone to lean on. He was a co-worker (who is still a friend of ours), and man-oh-man, would he learn to regret getting involved with me! We can laugh about it now, but he wasn't laughing on those nights he spent sleeping in his living room, facing his front door with a pistol in his hands. My brief affair ended up being the catalyst for my seeking an attorney, and fast!

Eugene's mother and brother were living with us at the time. Eugene was suspicious of the time I was spending with co-workers after work, so he had his mother get into my computer where they found proof of my affair. That day at work, I knew, from looking at my computer files, that Eugene had discovered our correspondence. I was relieved that he knew and (naively) wasn't fearful of his reaction at all. I just left work at closing time and drove home. It was all going to finally end. I'd finally be free and the children would no longer be subjected to piles of beer cans and hidden marijuana, emotional outbursts and financial instability. Hallelujah!

When I got home and walked in the front door, I sure wasn't expecting what happened next! He confronted me just inside the door. I noticed he was drunk, and I calmly looked him in the eye and quietly said, "I know you know." He then became verbally violent and emotionally unstable, screaming at me to leave. While I walked to the bedroom, he turned to Alexandra (our daughter, age 7 at the time) and told her to hide my laptop computer (which belonged to my employer). He then resumed his screaming. To protect the children from hearing his rage, I quickly left, planning to return the next day after he had calmed down. His mother was there, so I wasn't concerned for the children's safety. That was the biggest mistake of my life.

I drove to my parents' house while, at our house, Eugene sat the children down (ages 5, 7 and 11 at that time) and told them that I went to live with my boyfriend and that they wouldn't see me until Christmas. This was in July. You can imagine how distraught the children were. My youngest son is still suffering from the effects of that night.

When I left my children there, I stupidly assumed that their father would keep their best interests in mind. Instead, he tortured them, emotionally, to wound me. His actions then and those that followed would later cost him custody. It would also cost him the respect and love of his children once they realized, in therapy, what he did to them that night and why.

Later that evening, I spoke to the children by phone and told them I was at my parents' house, and that I'd be back the following day. He lied, telling them I would not be back. They didn't know whom to believe.

What Leaving Could Have Resulted In

The next day, my mom took me to an attorney who ordered me to return to the house immediately. If I was gone for more than 24 hours, Eugene could have claimed to the court that I abandoned the children. Leaving for just 24 hours could have cost me custody of my children! I've since learned that this is true in some states.

I did return, and Eugene met me at the door, blocking my path and refusing me entry. I was armed, though. I had two police officers by my side. At the suggestion of my attorney, I went to the police station and told them what was going on. They accompanied me to our house and explained to Eugene that he couldn't force me to leave my own home.

The police left and Eugene started following me through the house, with the children on his heels, screaming at the top of his lungs, "LEAVE! GO! LEAVE! GO!" He wouldn't stop. He didn't care that his actions were severely frightening the children. He only cared about hurting me and getting me out of the house. My youngest son (age 5 at that time) was trying to protect me by standing between us. He still blames himself for forgetting to lock the bedroom door, enabling Eugene to get inside.

Once inside the bedroom, Eugene told the children he had a videotape of me having sex with my boyfriend. He was lying, of course, but the children, again, didn't know whom to believe. He even offered to show them the tape. They didn't know what to say when he shouted, "Don't you want to see Mommy having sex with her boyfriend?!"

This was severe emotional abuse and I finally had to call 9-1-1. The police came and ordered Eugene to stay on one side of the house and me on the other. His mother, who had been present but silent during his tirade, said, "I'm leaving!" And, she did. She and Eugene's brother moved out of the house shortly thereafter.

Things became more unstable and dangerous the next day, and the next. Eugene engaged me in car chases. He tried to run me off the road in our neighborhood (the police call this vehicular assault). He chased me down another road and got out at a stoplight to bang on my windows while surrounded by other cars and motorists. When the light turned green, I stomped on the accelerator. I remember shaking so badly with fright that my foot was vibrating against the accelerator, making it difficult to drive at a steady speed. In my rearview mirror, I saw another car quickly pull in front of Eugene's car and stop, preventing him from chasing me further. A man, who saw what was happening (and who I will never be able to thank), stopped the chase by simply deciding to get involved. Even though he didn't know me, and despite the fact that it was obviously a very dangerous situation, he stepped in. To this day, I often think of that man and say a prayer for him.

An hour later, I was sitting in the police station typing up my complaint. I filed the police reports and, the next day, my attorney went to work to obtain a protective order. Eugene had refused to move out of the house. Instead, he kept the children and me up for hours each night, yelling.

One night in particular, he called our oldest son out of bed and threw a magazine at him. Eugene said, "Look at the smut your mother reads! She is sick in the head!" The magazine was Cosmopolitan. That's just one example of the psychological barrage he hurled at the children and me. They were all so frightened, yet so confused.

A few days later, unbeknownst to Eugene, I went to court with my attorney and the judge immediately granted the protective order. That afternoon, I picked the children up from school and checked into a hotel under a false name. I have never been so frightened in my life. I was terrified that he would get served with the order and hunt me down.

Eugene arrived home that evening and didn't know where we were. The police had been driving by, waiting for him to get home, and they served him with the order. He had 12 hours to move his belongings out of the house, and he was ordered to stay away from us. He moved to a vacant house in Liberty, Texas, a couple of hours away, which his father owned.

When I returned to the house with the children the following day, we were shocked. On opening the door, it looked like we'd been robbed. Eugene had dumped the contents of drawers out on the floor and left items, clothes, toys and more strewn all over the house. It took several days to put everything in order. The children were quite shaken by the sight. But, they would never again have to lie awake at night listening to Daddy scream at Mommy. That day was the beginning of the end.

If you obtain a protective order, obey it! Do not let him see the children if he's not allowed to!

Eugene was quite persuasive in making me feel sorry for him and, stupidly, I met him, outside the city limits, so he could see the children. That was a huge mistake. It was bad for the children because they knew the judge said he couldn't see them...yet Mommy was letting them go with him. And, of course, he used the opportunity to manipulate the children, lie to them, and make them even more emotionally unstable. I look back at some of my decisions during that time and can't believe how stupid I was. But, there was nobody there to tell me how things should be done.

If you have a protective order, don't let your spouse manipulate you. Don't accept his phone calls, either, as this not only gives him an emotional link and make him want to keep contacting you, but increases the chances that you'll fall victim to his manipulation. And, never do things against court order. Doing so will look very bad in court later. After all, if you feel your spouse is dangerous enough to obtain a protective order, why are you meeting with him? Why are you allowing the children to see him? The court may think you lied to obtain the protective order. You do not want the court to assume you're the dishonest party in your dispute, no matter how good your intentions are.

Where to Find Help When You Need It Most

Melinda W. Vasil

When a separation occurs in a marriage, it's often the wife who is left with little resources, lower income, and the task of raising the children, at least temporarily, without support from her husband.

Statistics show, year after year, that women of divorce have substantially less income than their husbands. As a result, the standard of living for divorced women and their children usually declines after the father leaves the home. Also, children of divorced parents have an automatic material disadvantage to their peers from intact families in the amount of support for education and extracurricular activities they are able to participate in, and have been shown to be in need of more financial assistance in their own marriages later in life.

While many men today are taking a more active role in their children's lives, even after divorce some seem to feel that, until a court order is issued, they are not obligated to assist in feeding, clothing, and sheltering their children.

What is a newly single mother to do when she suddenly finds herself in dire straits financially? There are many organizations set up to help in these situations, many of which most people are unaware.

If a woman finds herself without shelter, due to abuse in the marriage which leads her to flee with her children, or for any other reason, she should contact her local law enforcement agency (the police department) and get information on emergency housing. Any law enforcement agency should be able to point her in the direction of the local organization that can provide temporary housing in emergency situations. Many towns have Battered Women's Shelters that offer security and protection from the abuser, and are in secret locations to protect the residents. In addition, the local law enforcement can help obtain restraining/protective orders against the abuser if there is a threat of continued abuse.

Refer to the contact information for the National Domestic Abuse Hotline on page xiii for assistance with housing, legal, and financial aid.

After securing safe housing, the next order of business should be requesting a Child Support Order as soon as possible after the absent parent leaves the home or the children are otherwise left in a one-parent environment. The court will order temporary child support payments long before divorce proceedings are initiated. Courts

> *Some men seem to feel that, until a court order is issued, they are not obligated to assist in feeding, clothing, and sheltering their children.*

recognize that children's food and other needs can't wait while parents hammer out the details in court. Once you receive contact information for a local agency from the National Domestic Abuse Hotline, ask them for help in obtaining a temporary Child Support Order.

Every state has a Division of Social Services or Child Support Enforcement Office that can be contacted and that will assist with child support enforcement with no cost to the custodial parent. There is no need to hire an attorney for a simple Child Support Order in this country. However, for separation and divorce proceedings, it is imperative that a woman has her *own* attorney, not one shared by her spouse. She should contact her local Legal Aid service to find free or reduced-rate attorneys in the area. Again, contact the National Domestic Abuse Hotline for a referral in your town.

Many women in America today have chosen to be stay-at-home mothers, foregoing their careers to be full-time homemakers. Others make much less than their spouses due to the continued state of the business world to pay women far less than their male counterparts. When a separation and/or divorce occurs these women can be left literally destitute – unable to even feed their children. In these situations, the local Salvation Army or Food Bank will be of great assistance. The Salvation Army can also provide clothing for those that are in need.

It is a hard and humiliating step to take when picking up the phone to ask for help, but that is why these organizations exist, and no one will condemn or look down upon a woman seeking help. In fact, these organizations admire women who are taking steps to protect themselves and their children. Some may also provide leads to job opportunities that could lead to quicker independence from the system! They can also instruct you on how to obtain food stamps. The local federal agency that handles food stamps in your area will probably give you immediate assistance and will then mail weekly food stamps to you in an amount based on your family's needs.

If a woman is unemployed, she should contact her local Employment Security Commission or Job Assistance Association and file an application for employment. She should also inquire about childcare that may be available for free or on a sliding scale until she is established in her job, if needed. Many local churches provide such child care services. Head Start is another government-sponsored program designed for children of low-income families to provide childcare and early learning programs for the disadvantaged in public schools. Parents of low-income families can learn more about these programs through their local Social Services Department.

The most important thing for any woman in this situation to remember is that she is not alone. There are, unfortunately, millions of other women who are or have been in the same boat. The services mentioned here were developed for just such situations, and are available for free to anyone who needs them. Do not be afraid or ashamed to take the actions necessary to provide for your children and yourself. In the United States, there should be no reason for a child to go hungry, unsheltered, or unclothed due to financial hardships in the family.

What You Must Find and Hide Right Now

Angela Hoy

Eugene had, in his possession, two nude photographs of me that I had taken of myself, for him, years earlier during happier times. During the divorce, Eugene showed these photographs to the children and to other people as well, and lied, telling everyone I'd taken the pictures for my boyfriend.

Had I been thinking straight, I'd have found these and destroyed or hidden them before the marriage imploded. But, most women aren't pre-meditative in nature so we don't make plans to deceive. However, you're about to declare war and it's time to prepare. You need to secure your arsenal and protect your assets.

Things to hide or destroy before you ask for a divorce:

Any item he may use to embarrass you later on such as diaries, journals, emails, letters, etc. – Eugene stole my computer, which belonged to my employer. Getting it back was a legal hassle and was quite embarrassing for me at work. Eugene threatened to use emails (that I had sent to my boyfriend from that computer) when fighting for custody of the children. Had I anticipated his Divorce Psychosis, I'd have left my laptop computer in my locked car instead of carrying it into the house each evening.

Any sentimental items that he may take for value or spite – I left all the photos albums at the house when I took the children to a hotel while Eugene was served with the protective order. He took the photo albums when he left. And, while I agree that he was entitled to some of the pictures, I feel that most of them belong to the children so they can pass them along to their children someday. I ended up with most of the videotapes (he left those behind), but I really wish we had more photographs. I know the children will never recover those.

I also had a doll my father gave to me before he died (when I was 5). Eugene threw my doll away when he was angry with me one day. I wish I'd hidden that doll long before things started to sour.

Weapons – The first question the police asked me each time they came to our house to diffuse situations was if there were any weapons in the house. You absolutely must hide or discard of all weapons, including guns, ammunition, knives, or any item that could be used to harm you or your children.

Any embarrassing pictures or videos of yourself and any adult or sexual items that you don't want your ex's attorney waving in your face in a courtroom. Let's face it. Many couples enjoy creative sex lives. We just don't talk about it to our neighbors and children. And, no matter how innocent your actions and adult possessions seem at the time, and no matter how much you loved your spouse when you utilized these things, they will no longer seem so innocent when they're entered as evidence in a child custody hearing. Many shunned spouses portray these items as evil mechanisms that depict their owners as twisted fiends (even if the spouse used the items, too!). Think about what you possess that may cause embarrassment or harm to you in court. Find these items and hide or destroy them.

Do These Things <u>Before</u> You Say the Word 'Divorce'

Angela Hoy

Once you've made the decision to get divorced, your entire life will turn into a nasty game of word play and manipulation. Rather than letting the big bang occur all at once, in a fit of rage, it's a good idea to have things prepared first.

If you're considering divorce, **call the police if you're having an argument and you're frightened**. Police reports carry a lot more weight in court than his word versus yours. I can't express how valuable these police reports will be to you later during the legal process. Some states even award additional support to spouses who were the victims of physical abuse.

Immediately contact your children's schools. Not only do they need to know that your child may require emotional support during this time, but they also need to know who is permitted to pick up your child and who is not. They will not refuse to release your child to his father unless you have a protective or custody order in hand. Be prepared.

If your spouse is abusive, or unstable in any way, you should **obtain a protective order prior to telling him you want a divorce**. At this time, any police reports concerning domestic violence will encourage the judge to grant a protective order. Your spouse will probably not be told of this action until after the order is issued. This helps to ensure the safety of the victim filing for protection. The police (or another court-appointed person) will serve your spouse with the order. It's a good idea for you to be in hiding when this occurs because you do not know what his reaction will be.

This is also a good idea if he's abusive and you think he's going to try to fight for custody. Having a protective order in place protects you and the children from him for several days (until the judge schedules a hearing) and will probably also provide you with custody during that period, provided the protective order instructs him to stay away from you and the children. The judge may be more likely to later give continued custody to the spouse who already has custody.

Request a restraining order as well. A restraining order is different from a protective order. (Different states have different names for these items.) A restraining order protects the marital assets and will prevent you and him from cleaning out the bank accounts. Funds can then only be used for necessary items, such as groceries, utilities, etc. Warning – He will probably still wipe out the bank accounts. Many people suffering from Divorce Psychosis are more intent on inflicting emotional, financial and physical pain on their spouse than they are about obeying court orders. Be prepared for this!

Open your own bank account <u>now</u>. Start depositing your paychecks and any funds (welfare, etc.) into your own bank account. This will prevent him from taking your money later.

Secure all items that you don't want your spouse to take. Hide them, take them to your mother's or a friend's or destroy them. Some people have been known to burn down the family home during a divorce. Others know exactly what to use in court against their spouse, or take joy in revenge by destroying or selling family heirlooms.

Get rid of all guns and other weapons in the house! I asked my brother-in-law to hide my husband's guns in the woods behind our house after things started getting bad. That was at the suggestion of the police. If he was willing to run me off the road and puncture my tire, what was he capable of? Assume the worst!

Arrange for emergency shelter. Find a friend, family member or shelter willing to house you in the event of an emergency. Tell them you may need to come by spur of the moment. Don't tell anyone on his side of the family or, of course, any friends (you never know what mutual friends will tell someone during a divorce) where your safe-haven is. If you must stay with someone your spouse knows, hide your car elsewhere so he won't know you're there. I once asked a friend to meet me at another location so I could leave my car hidden in a parking lot.

Pack a bag of necessities (clothes, toys for the children, snacks, drinks, and copies of important papers) and keep it hidden in your trunk. This enables you to run out the door without needing to grab anything. Keep a spare key hidden inside the car so you will be able to get away even if he takes your keys or if you don't have time to grab them when fleeing. Unless you have several children who may need to flee simultaneously with you, keep all doors locked except the driver's door so you can protect yourself quickly if he is chasing you.

Keep copies of all court orders hidden in your house and additional copies in your car. If the police are summoned, you'll need to be able to provide them with a copy to prove your spouse is violating those orders. After I drove to the police department one night, I had to drive back to my house to get a copy of our restraining order for the police. While I was in the house, Eugene punctured my tire, right in front of the children. I then had to drive back to the police station on the rim of the wheel. He chased me in his car and he'd placed all the children in the car with him. And, of course, he was drunk. If I'd kept a copy of the order in my car, that evening would not have been so traumatic for the children.

Talk to your children. Tell them everything that's happening. This is not the time to cover your children's eyes and ears. They hear the arguments and they'll be much stronger during the process if they're informed. Wondering who is hiding what from them does irreparable damage to young minds. Knowledge and honesty are the keys to their recovery from this difficult time in their lives.

You want your children to hear the truth from you <u>before</u> they hear lies from your spouse or others (your in-laws). And, tell them your spouse will probably lie to them about you to hurt you (not to intentionally hurt them). Then, they'll be prepared and will not believe everything he says about you and the unstable situation. Be truthful. Never lie to your children. They'll find out later about any lies and will lose faith in the parent who told them those lies.

None of the contributors in this book suspected in any way what lengths their spouses would go to in harming them and their children, physically, financially, and emotionally. Expect the worse from your spouse, because that's probably what you're going to get.

Ask the Police for Help Before the War Begins

Angela Hoy

Each year, when we're going on vacation, I alert the police department that we're leaving. They're happy to drive by periodically to check on things while we're gone.

Likewise, if you're going to ask for a divorce, you need to alert the police of your plans and ask them to keep an eye on your house. This is as simple as calling the receptionist at the police station and saying, "I'm about to ask my husband for a divorce and I wanted to ask your officers to keep an eye on my house and to be alert for anything out of the ordinary." Be sure to tell them if you suspect your spouse may react with violence. Police officers are trained to notice suspicious things that may indicate a problem, such as a car parked half in the driveway, half in the yard indicating someone in a hurry, broken windows, children acting odd while outside, etc.

What can you expect from your spouse once you ask for a divorce? Well, you can expect the common forms of grief, such as anger and denial. But, you should also expect irrational behavior such as:

· Cleaning out and closing of bank accounts

· Brain washing/lies to children

· Possible kidnapping

· Suicide threats/attempts

· Threats/attempts to kill/beat you and/or your children and other family members

· Theft of sentimental and valuable items

· Threats to your employer or your job security. My ex threatened to sue my employer for contributing to the failure of his marriage. Bizarre as it sounds, my employer had to contact the local constable and lock the office doors daily for quite awhile because of Eugene's unpredictable behavior. This may have been his attempt to make me lose my job, thus ensuring I couldn't support the children so he might get custody. It didn't work, but it very well could have. Don't be surprised if your spouse tries to make you lose your job.

· Unreasonable demands such as requesting odd visitation terms (taking only one child at a time or deviating from the visitation schedule), asking for sex "just one last time", asking for a loan (don't give him any money!), frequent phone calls, nice or not, to try to maintain some kind of emotional connection with you, or anything that seems the least bit uncomfortable, bizarre, or unfair to you and the children.

The Ex Files -
Documentation During the Divorce Process

Beth Airey

Now that you are in the process of divorce, it's important to build your position of legal strength by constructing what attorneys sometimes call a "paper fortress." Divorce documentation includes proof or record of *anything* that could be even remotely used to support your case for divorce, custody, or child support, or that may impact the property settlement that is awarded.

Examples of such documentation would include:

· Phone conversations (Laws pertaining to taping conversations vary by state, so check with your attorney.) - A summary of wiretapping laws by state can be found at http://www.rcfp.org/taping/states.html, or search for "wire tapping laws" in your favorite search engine. If you can't tape phone conversations, take detailed notes of what is said, and include the date and time of each phone call in your records.

· Telephone answering machine/voice mail messages

· Letters

· E-mails (both the ones you send and the ones you receive)

· Written, dated records of conversations (and arguments or threats) and their outcomes

· Written, dated records of visitations and any other incidents concerning the children, even if they go smoothly or are otherwise uneventful. Always make note of when your spouse is late, cancels or doesn't show up for scheduled visitation.

· Financial records, such as titles, bank statements, canceled checks, insurance policies, and copies of bills that may be necessary in court.

You'll need a few supplies to effectively and efficiently handle your divorce documentation. First, purchase several file folders and a large wire-bound notebook. (Or, if money is tight, you can create a notebook using your children's loose-leaf notebook paper.) Next, if you don't already have an answering machine or voice mail system, get one right away. A service such as CallNotes (ask your local phone company for help) can be very effective since it will take messages while the phone is busy. In case you need to tape telephone conversations, purchase a cassette recorder and microphone. Your local electronics or office supply store or even Walmart® can help with this.

Here are recommendations for divorce documentation:

· As soon as something relevant occurs or materializes, write it down, print it out, toss it in the file or make a cassette recording of it *right away*. Procrastination is the enemy of this mission. The more documentation you accumulate, the more ammunition you'll have in court.

· Make sure your records are hidden and secure.

· When in doubt, document anyway.

But there's more that you need to know when it comes to building a rock-solid foundation of legal proof. Read on:

Do begin documenting your situation immediately. Haven't been documenting so far? Don't put it off one more day. Start right away, and begin by compiling and writing down what facts you can recall about your marriage and spouse, and rounding up correspondence and copies of bills and statements.

Don't make the mistake of thinking that you won't need supporting documents because your soon-to-be-ex is being civil. People experiencing a divorce can change very quickly and a friendly situation can become volatile overnight. Never, ever release your documentation to your spouse or tell him that it even exists.

Do think of divorce as the audit that never ends. You wouldn't dream of tossing a piece of paper or forgetting a fact that might be called into question by the IRS. Treat the divorce process with the same importance.

Don't show your cards when it comes to documentation. Did he say something very incriminating on your answering machine? Tape it and keep it. Did he send a heinous e-mail? Save it and print it out. Remember to keep these facts to yourself, which will maximize their legal impact should their use become necessary. Mention the incidents during your next conference with your attorney.

Do remember that your spouse is probably stockpiling documents on you, too! Mind your manners on the phone, via e-mail, and in letters. Don't say or do anything you wouldn't want to have entered as evidence in a court of law.

Don't end the paper trail when the divorce decree is signed. Plan on continuing your documentation efforts indefinitely after the divorce, particularly when there are children involved. Custody could come up again (some men decide to sue for custody years after the divorce) and child support may be late or not paid at all.

Do keep your box of files and other documentation stored away where you can't see it. This is to keep you from wasting your emotional energy by getting a knot in your stomach every time you see it, or from getting yourself all worked up when you view evidence of unsavory events. This is disruptive to your healing process, so keep your documentation out of sight.

Why You Should Hide Your Documentation

Angela Hoy

My ex-husband, Eugene, made the mistake of keeping all of his documentation in his car. In that documentation were the two nude photos I mentioned in an earlier chapter. One morning, as we were on our way to a meeting with a marriage counselor (I was trying to have a third party convince him to be more civil during the divorce for the children's sake), I found his envelope of documentation under the front seat of his car. With glee, I grabbed it, jumped in my own car, raced to my office, and locked it in a cabinet. I then calmly drove to the counselor's office around the corner and waited for him to arrive.

He met me there and I knew right away that he knew what I'd done. He was in a RAGE! The counselor, an elderly woman, was quite frightened by his violent behavior. He entered her office, grabbed my purse, screamed at me, and walked out. Luckily, I'd anticipated this reaction. Otherwise, the documentation may have been in my car and he'd have gotten it back. While he did later return my purse under the advice of his attorney (more on his "attorney" later), he had a friend drive my vehicle into downtown Houston and hide it in a parking garage. I had to rely on friends until I obtained other transportation.

Eugene never did get those pictures back. (And, honestly, I still laugh when I think about that day.) After he left, a friend picked me up and I returned to my office and immediately cut those pictures up into thousands of pieces.

So, my lesson to you here is, if you have something important, hide it…and not under the car seat!

Alcoholism/Drug Abuse = Get Out!
Enabling Only Makes it Worse!

Angela Hoy

Co-dependent and enabler. If you've read articles or books on alcoholism, you probably know these terms. A common problem in families dealing with alcoholism or drug addiction is that the spouse of the addict will enable the addict to continue in the destructive behavior by helping them deal with the consequences of their actions.

These can include:

· Helping them wake up in the morning when they have a hangover

· Making up excuses for their behavior to families, bosses and government agencies (police, children's protective services)

· Bailing them out of jail

· Physically cleaning up their messes

· Lying to the insurance company after accidents

When Eugene had hangovers, I often called his employers to tell them he was sick and couldn't come to work. I lied to family and friends about why we were late to events and made excuses for his odd behavior when he was intoxicated.

Once, Eugene was reported to Children's Protective Services (CPS) because the police found our youngest son outside, twice in one morning, alone in his diaper. I was at work that day. CPS interviewed me later that week and I lied, telling them that Eugene's story about being on medication for a backache was true.

One time, right after we were married, I told the truth to his boss (who called me at my office) about why he didn't go to work that day. He hadn't shown up for a meeting because he was still in bed. Eugene got fired the same day. He was furious with me for doing that and I learned quickly to lie just to keep the peace.

Years later, another boss of his (an old friend of ours) called me at work to ask if Eugene was an alcoholic. I said yes. He later lost that job, too, but he claimed it was for different reasons.

I bailed him out of jail twice, once when he was arrested for Driving While Intoxicated (DWI) and once for driving with a suspended license. His DWI case was dismissed after the judge determined he had not been given a complete field sobriety test. The police officer allegedly arrested Eugene, after he rear-ended another vehicle, after only making him do a portion of the field test. Eugene told me the officer said, "I can smell it on your breath," and arrested him. My parents paid for Eugene's attorney, so they enabled his drinking, too, at my pleading.

I often screamed in his ear and occasionally poured water on him to get him to wake up and go to work when he had a hangover. He would eventually get up and then turn on the shower, lie down in the shower, and go back to sleep under the spray. While trying to get myself ready for work and the children ready for school, I'd have to keep yelling at him, pleading for him to not lose another job.

I even got up countless times in the middle of the night to clean his urine off the floor when he was too drunk to find the bathroom.

My ex-mother-in-law also always seemed to enable her children's destructive behavior. She willingly gave money when they needed it, bailed them out of jail, and sat by painfully watching their drunken stupors and foolish behavior. During our divorce, she allowed Eugene to stay at her house one night, drunk, which, I was told, resulted in a fistfight between him and his brother.

His brother, also convicted more than once for driving while intoxicated, was sentenced to jail. His mother told me the court then ordered a breathalyzer device be installed on his brother's car that won't allow the car to start if there is too much alcohol in his system. She then told me he filled up a balloon with air when he was sober, carried the balloon with him, and expelled that air into the machine whenever he'd been drinking, thus enabling him to drink and drive yet again. The last I heard, her other son was still living with her, though he's almost 40 years old.

I must share something here about my ex-brother-in-law. He was incredible with kids and the children loved him dearly. He never hesitated to drop everything if someone needed him, including me. He lived with us for a period of time and was our "nanny" for several months. He was there the night Eugene poured beer on my keyboard and he was also living with us when the divorce process began.

During the divorce, before the protective order was granted, I was caving under the pressure by Eugene to get back together with him. I kept saying no, but inside I wasn't sure if I was strong enough to go through with the divorce. Apparently, Eugene told his mother we might reconcile.

That night, my brother-in-law said, "Mom says you two might get back together. If you do, you're the stupidest person I know."

That one statement was a huge eye-opener for me and was the deciding factor to remain separated and pursue the divorce. If Eugene's own brother agreed that I should divorce him, I must be doing the right thing.

I have often pitied my ex-mother-in-law when I realize that her entire life revolves around her children and how much pain alcohol and drugs have brought to her. I was determined that my golden years would not be spent enabling my children, should they choose to abuse alcohol or drugs.

I wish now that I'd not enabled Eugene's alcoholism, allowing it to rule almost every aspect of our lives. I wish I'd just left him in bed in the morning and worried about getting myself to work and the children to school. I wish I'd told the truth to that CPS worker. I wish I'd never lied to his bosses, family, and friends on so many occasions. If I'd let him deal with all the consequences of his actions by himself, my life would have been much easier during those 12½ years. I'd have not spent 12½ years wasting energy and worrying about something I could not control.

Alcoholism apparently runs in Eugene's family and also in mine. My maternal grandmother was also an alcoholic. So, I read that my children have a 50% or greater chance of becoming alcoholics. How could I stop alcoholism from destroying their lives and their future families' lives as well? Getting a divorce and custody was one way of attempting to stop the cycle of the disease in our family.

Breaking the Co-Dependent Bond

Linda Goin

In my late twenties, I was lonely and looking for love in a neighborhood bar. It wasn't long before I met a man who agreed to help me create a fearful bond of alcoholism and abusive behavior. After one year of marriage, I was hired by an alcohol rehabilitation center. Over the next three years, I learned more about this disease than most doctors learn in a lifetime. For example, women attracted to men with addictive behaviors often have low self-esteem. These women also tend to lose touch with their feelings and with the skill to communicate. The person who lives with an alcoholic - also known as a "co-alcoholic" or "co-dependent" - often denies any problems exist and tries to hide the drinking problem from friends and family. The person who lives with an alcoholic is a drunk without a bottle, because they eventually develop the same behaviors as the alcoholic.

One year after I married my bar buddy, he was hospitalized after experiencing a seizure at work. I rushed to his side to find him suffering with full-blown delirium tremens. I understood everything my husband said during his hallucinations. This frightened me and forced me to wonder about my own sanity.

The hospital staff wasn't equipped to deal with alcohol withdrawals, so they transferred my husband to a local treatment center. This center conducted a "family week" during the third week of their month-long treatment program. This week was designed to teach family members about the disease of alcoholism through classes and group therapy with the patients. My husband's parents refused to participate, but I found myself looking forward to this week. Through the help of the counselors, I finally understood how my emotional problems stemmed from this disease.

My husband refused to acknowledge his problem. At the end of family week, he was discharged for his disruptive behavior. He threatened me with bodily harm if I didn't leave with him. I knew if I left, I would probably die by his hand or by my own. I was convinced I couldn't live with this marriage any longer. The counselors asked me to stay at the center, and I was grateful for the invitation. Later that month, the center hired me and transferred me to another city.

> *I convinced myself I didn't fight for my rights simply because I wanted out of the marriage. It would take another year of therapy before I learned about assertive behavior!*

I asked for a divorce before I left town. My husband's parents were defensive about the divorce. They were afraid I would try to "take" their son for "everything he had." This was ludicrous, since my husband no longer had a job, a place to live, or any money. Somehow, my husband and his parents convinced me I didn't need an attorney. As a result, I left many personal belongings behind. I convinced myself I didn't fight for my rights simply because I wanted out of the marriage. It would take another year of therapy before I learned about assertive behavior!

Was there a way to avoid this disaster? I doubt it. If I knew about the behaviors of this disease, behaviors that are often passed down through generations, I might have recognized a pattern within my own family. Since the keystone symptom of this disease is denial, I'm not sure I would have acknowledged the information. Sometimes we need to live with the emotional and physical destruction of alcoholism so we can learn to help others.

If you want to avoid this scenario, you need to do two things. First, you need to research the drinking patterns of your family and your partner's family. If you detect heavy drinkers hanging out on the branches of either family tree (Oh, your Uncle Harry drank like a fish!), then you need to learn more about the disease. The Internet didn't exist during my marriage, but you probably have access to this resource. Type "alcoholism" into any search engine and you'll find a wealth of information on behaviors and treatment. The second thing you need to do is to never marry a man you meet in a bar.

Oh, one more bit of advice - if you go through a divorce without your own attorney, go find a course in assertiveness training. You'll need it just to get over the shame and remorse.

Think He'll Stop Drinking? Think Again!

Lois Wheatley

With all the compassion that properly should be accorded to an alcoholic, it truly is a chronic disease that only a rare few ever beat.

I put my husband into five (count 'em - five) in-patient rehab programs. It worked according to the law of diminishing returns. After his first stay, he was sober for two years, a fabulous two years, probably the best of my life. After his second stay, he was sober for about two months. Following his third stay, he behaved himself for maybe two weeks, and the fourth stay won me about two days.

His fifth stint was in one of the best programs I'd seen, in a non-hospital setting with family counseling and a scenic countryside. When he got home, it took him about two hours to unpack, shower, change, and find the car keys. Somehow he must have known this was my cue to get on down the road, because he made it impossible for me to do otherwise. He slept by day while I worked and, when I came home, conducted all-night rituals of screamings, beatings, rapings, chasing me around the house with a gun, and more.

I dialed 9-1-1 and reported being raped. When you file rape charges, the physical exam is a requirement for forensic evidence, which involves a full pelvic exam and, my favorite, the plucking of about 10 or so pubic hairs, which I could just imagine a judge in chambers examining closely for signs of consent. I knew a restraining order would not be worth the paper it was printed on, and he would have plans for that gun collection of his.

While he was in jail, I rented a trailer and packed up my two-year-old daughter. We headed out from our Virginia home to the suburbs of Atlanta, Georgia, a journey of about a thousand miles that simply wasn't far enough. I stayed with an old friend from high school until I could find a job and a place to live.

The rape case was dropped for lack of a witness and he tracked me down in no time flat. Trouble was, I wasn't home when he figured out where I lived, so he had to break in. And since the original goal was to inflict damage on me in any way possible, he picked up some cash and a few minor possessions.

> *My lawyer suggested a sneaky, underhanded method of dealing with the situation that would make everyone happy.*

Again I dialed 9-1-1. This time I was dealing with the Georgia police, and they told me about an interesting law in the state of Georgia. A woman who is still legally married is her husband's chattel, and her home is his home. Her cash and minor possessions are his cash and minor possessions. The man was within his rights. "Go for nonsupport," they said. "We take a dim view of nonsupport here in these parts. But you'll need a custody and support order first."

I hired an attorney who threw back his head and laughed when I told him of my meager efforts to hide my whereabouts, which amounted to little more than the glasses, nose, and moustache disguise. He said, "Even a bad detective can find you if you have a phone and utilities in your name."

In retrospect, I have no idea what I could have done differently with that...move in with a roommate, I guess. My lawyer made no headway whatsoever in negotiations with my husband, who threw a pitched battle when and if he deemed fit to address the issue at all. Contested divorces usually cost twice the money in legal fees, and take about three to four times as long.

My lawyer suggested a sneaky, underhanded method of dealing with the situation that would make everyone happy. He took out a notice in a legal publication that circulated in northern Georgia. It ran for three consecutive months and he followed that up with a petition for divorce that claimed, truthfully, that my husband had been notified of the proceedings via registered mail. My lazy husband responded to that registered letter about six months later, and it was a done deal by that time.

I had the divorce decree in hand for the next assault he would launch. The ironic twist to this whole story is that the next assault never happened. The next thing I heard was from his parents, begging me to go to the hospital where he was in the critical care ward. Kidney, liver, stomach - it was like a sidewalk sale. Everything must go. The doctors gave him zero odds. I went and took our daughter. He died a week or so after that, at the ripe old age of 38. He never even found out he was divorced.

What Staying May Be Doing to Your Children

Angela Hoy

After the children's last visit with Eugene, I had to put them all into counseling to deal with the neglect they'd experienced while there. Eugene had slept a great deal of the time, broken promises and put them in uncomfortable and dangerous situations. That trip was especially hard on Alexandra, who was 10½ at that time.

The first therapist, in Massachusetts, told me that Alexandra had no self-esteem. No, not "low" self-esteem…no self-esteem. Why is that? I've been telling her how beautiful and smart she is since the day she was born. The therapist speculated there were two possible reasons:

1. She was Daddy's Little Girl for eight years of her life. She adored him. She worshipped him. And, for most of those eight years, through his actions, she was given the unspoken message that alcohol was more important than her.

2. She watched her mother (me) bow down and consent to everything bad occurring in our home just to keep the peace. I unknowingly taught Alexandra that women must be submissive and that they have no right to speak up when something is wrong. Alexandra knows that women don't count in this world and that men hold all the cards. I taught her that, and I will have to live with that for the rest of my life. And, she will be subconsciously affected by my weaknesses for the rest of her life.

The therapist started behavior therapy with Alexandra so she would learn how to "esteem herself." She was given a notebook to write in and she had to answer questions daily about what is good about Alexandra, what Alexandra did great today, why Alexandra is proud of herself, etc.

But, this was just the beginning. It will be years, and perhaps never, until Alexandra learns that she has a voice in the world and that her voice counts. The damage has been done…over and over again for eight long years.

31

> *Nobody told me that staying was the worst possible thing for my children.*

If you are in an abusive relationship, <u>you must get out</u>. By staying, you may be allowing long-term and probably permanent damage to your children's emotional health.

My mistake? Staying for 12½ years. Why did I stay? Everyone said to stick it out for the children. Nobody told me that staying was the worst possible thing for my children.

More Advice to <u>Not</u> Stay Together
for the Children

Lynnemarie Casaregola

There were a lot of hidden secrets my mother did not know about my father and his family before they got married. They had only dated a year before the wedding. In retrospect, my mother didn't really know the man she was marrying at all. She started finding these things out on her honeymoon.

My father was born with a birth defect and only had one hand. The other was a stump with tiny bumps that should have been fingers. My mother didn't care. She loved him, not his hand. My mother later found out that, when my father was growing up, his family made him hide his hand when meeting new people or at any social occasions.

Every time I pulled my camera out he would get annoyed and tell me not to take his picture. I never really realized the psychological damage that was done to him by his family, or maybe I just didn't want to know. When I was little, I saw his baby pictures and, in them, his hand was always hidden. At his wake, "the family" made the funeral director hide his hand in the casket. I was outraged by this and could see why my father could never have a good marriage with anyone.

Several years before my parents met, my father was in a near-fatal car accident, and the friend he was with died in his arms. It was at that point when his phobia of not being able to drive by himself, except for the small areas around town, started. It lasted until the day he died. He always carpooled to work, or my mother would drive him. That was just one of many secrets my mother discovered after the marriage. Dad was also a controlled alcoholic who hid it well, but not well enough for my mother not to notice how much beer he consumed every night.

When they first married, they lived around the corner from my grandmother and across the street from his sister. I was conceived in Catskill, New York, but my mother made Dad move to Coxsackie, which was only twenty minutes away from his interfering family. Dad didn't want a big family and, after I was born, he didn't want to have any more kids. My mom wanted at least two more children and felt like she had been lied to. I guess she had been. When I look back now, it is a good thing she didn't have any more children. They were spared the torment of that dysfunctional household.

At one point, when I was six years old, Dad went to see a psychologist. He ended up going for two years. My mother said their marriage improved and she was actually happy. Mom would sit in on some of the sessions and the psychologist confirmed what Mom already knew. Dad's family was responsible for his phobias and, indirectly, the drinking. Dad drank to take the pain away, the pain that was caused by his abnormal upbringing.

My mother made a lethal mistake by telling my father's sister he was getting help. She, in turn, told "the family" and they forced Dad to stop seeking help because, if anyone where they lived found out, it would embarrass them. Of course, when he stopped therapy, the marriage began to spiral downhill. My father's family started to treat my mother badly, and he never stood up for her. They told her everything she did in raising me was wrong and that I was a spoiled brat. That was when my mother decided she would stay in the marriage until I was eighteen and then leave my father when I graduated from high school.

Time moved on and our family made the weekly Sunday visits to my father's family. His two brothers and sister were also there with their families. I could feel the tension between everyone there but just brushed it off and went to play outside. By the time I was thirteen, my mother was sleeping on the couch and my father remained in their bed.

Near the end of my senior year, my mother filed the separation papers. During my graduation ceremony, my father's family sat on the left side of the decorated gym while my mother's family sat on the right side. None of them talked, only glared at each other from across the room. That ruined my graduation totally. I had two separate parties that were both horrible. I was completely miserable at a time when I should have been overjoyed.

At the time of their divorce, my father's company, where he had worked for twenty-six years, was downsizing, and they gave him a small pay off. My father never recovered from this. His family frowned upon divorce and gave him very little support. His lack of confidence and hatred of life is what killed him in the end. He never took care of himself. He continued to drink and smoke heavily and stopped eating. I did everything I could to help and asked my aunt and uncles to help. They did nothing but ignore it and say he was fine. I am not a person who hides my feelings. I told my father's family very loudly exactly what

I thought of them right at the funeral parlor. Do I regret it? Not one bit, and I never will.

My mother told me her biggest mistake was not leaving the marriage when I was little, and I agree. She wished she knew all his secrets

> *My mother told me her biggest mistake was not leaving the marriage when I was little, and I agree.*

before they married. She didn't get to know the real man who carried a lifetime of problems that he hid well. She should have made sure he was her best friend and that they communicated and were truthful with each other. Her best advice is to avoid these mistakes. Get to know the person and their family before you decide to jump into the lifetime commitment of marriage.

Lynnemarie Casaregola has been published by Shape Magazine and is a Contributing Editor at Suite 101 on the topic Situation Comedies. She was formerly Contributing Editor on the topic, Appearances: Before and After. Lynnemarie Casaregola is a pen name she is using for this book.

In Only 24 Hours, You Could Lose Custody of Your Babies

Denise

"Get out of here! Go away! Just leave!"

My four-year-old daughter chanted in harmony with her father as I tearfully backed the car out of the driveway. My two-year-old son screamed because Mommy was leaving. It is a memory that still threatens to stop my heart.

This was the first night I was forced from my home but, unfortunately, it was not the last. Every time my husband and I had a disagreement, it ended with him telling me to just leave. At the time, I thought I was doing what was best for both the kids and myself. Now I know that my husband was playing a very serious game, and his victory depended on me not knowing the rules. My story did not have a happy ending, but yours could if you know the rules.

Stay in the home. I know you have heard that possession is nine-tenths of the law. Well, this rule applies for custody of children, too. If you leave your children with your husband while you go cool off, it could be considered abandonment in as little as 24 hours. One day to cool off is not very long, especially when emotions are running high. But, every time my husband forced me to leave, it was documented and used against me in court. Do what you can to encourage him to leave the house. Keep the kids in their own home and hold your ground.

Take the children with you. If you are in an abusive situation where you are concerned for the well being of the children and/or yourself, get out of there when your husband goes to work. You may need to leave quickly without many possessions, but the alternative is much worse. Be sure to get the advice of an attorney if you decide to do this. This was difficult for me because rural Nebraska has no shelters for abused women and my family was not supportive of a divorce.

If you are forced to leave, seek help immediately. One night I did refuse to leave the home. My husband invited both our parents to our fight. I became the piñata at this little party and was hauled to the hospital where my husband tried to have me committed, even though it was obvious to the hospital staff that my bleeding mouth was the color of an eggplant. I declined to press charges because they had broken me to the point where I believed I was the problem. I decided to check myself into the hospital for three days just to get some rest. Both of these decisions were terrible

> *Now I know that my husband was playing a very serious game, and his victory depended on me not knowing the rules.*

mistakes. When we went to court, there was no record of abuse and my mental capacities were called into question.

The final time I was expelled, I was nearly despondent from a year's worth of emotional stress. I did not fight him that day because I knew it would be a traumatic scene for the kids. I fled to my girlfriend's home and cried for two days. By that time, I decided to hire an attorney, but it was too late. I dialed every number in the phone book, but no one would help me fight for custody of my babies. The courts do not like to disrupt the lives of children unless they are abused. Since I left my children with my husband, it would be argued that I must have believed that was the best place for them. It did not matter that I fled because of the threat of violence or that his idea of caring for the kids was to dump them with his mother or his girlfriend.

Clearly, I made many mistakes during my divorce. I had some funny notions that integrity and logic would win in the end. I lost custody of my children because I was naïve. Get the facts from an attorney and act decisively for both the children and for yourself.

Denise is a freelance writer living in Lincoln, NE, who now has a wonderful relationship with her children.

Threatening to "Commit" You is a Common, Empty Threat

Angela Hoy

It is common for husbands to threaten to commit their wives to institutions or hospitals. In Denise's case, it is obvious that her husband had legal (though unethical) advice and each move on his part was a calculated action to obtain sole custody of their children. Obviously, making her leave the house to keep the peace was not in the best interests of their children.

I, too, thought that, if I left, Eugene would stop screaming. And, he would not allow me to take the children when I did leave. Luckily, I obtained legal advice quickly, before any damage was done.

Keep in mind that your spouse may already have legal representation and his actions and requests (no matter how reasonable they may seem at that moment) may result in you losing custody of your children.

Some men don't even want custody of their children. They only fight for custody to hurt the mother. And, if they have legal advice while the mother does not, they may win.

If your spouse threatens to commit you, contact an attorney. In fact, call any mental health facility and they'll tell you the guidelines for committing someone. They usually require a doctor's orders, plus a signature from the spouse _and_ another signature from someone on the "patient's" side of the family. Mental health facilities don't send out their ambulances on a whim every time a disgruntled spouse requests it.

Eugene threw that threat my way. And, honestly, it frightened me, until my attorney laughed and told me how hard it is to commit someone these days.

Think You're Not Being Psychologically Abused? Think Again!

Pauline

Bullies always want to make their wives think that they are brainless idiots, worthless, and that they should be thankful they have a man at all.

Every divorced woman I have ever talked to said they were told how stupid and brainless they were. They were made to feel so undesirable and totally unlovable that they ended up feeling that their own parents didn't really want them either (mine really didn't).

All of these things happened to me, but others have told me they heard the same things:

"Don't be stupid."

"Shut up. You're making a fool of yourself. No one wants to know what you think."

"What the hell did you do that for?"

"I don't want people to know our business. You keep away from her."

And to other people:

"Her? She doesn't have a clue. Shit for brains."

If your friends call the house and he answers the phone, he either doesn't let you know the friends called, or he makes filthy sexual suggestions to them over the phone so they won't call again. Also, in your friends' company, he tends to make crude remarks so the friends soon get the idea to keep away. This adds to your isolation and aids him in his psychological abuse.

Your parents keep quiet about their observations because they don't want to get caught up in it or they think you don't realize what he is doing. You should ask your friends if they called earlier and, if he answered, tell them he didn't (and won't) pass the messages on. You should <u>never</u> apologize for his behavior.

You should be on the lookout for odd accounts, missing clothes, in some cases underpants, and irritability when he doesn't want you to see the bank account, credit card receipts, or phone bills.

Call the police when he threatens to kill you, your parents, your children, or your dog, or threatens to commit suicide, etc.

If he starts issuing threats, <u>tell the police immediately</u>. They can't act if you haven't told them about the threats.

When the threat of suicide doesn't make you bend to his will, he may continue with vicious threats about killing or hurting you or someone you love.

These threats signify severe mental instability and must <u>not</u> be ignored. Make sure that someone is always watching your children. Do not let them wait outside school for you. If you can't pick them up on time, have them picked up and kept inside until you get home from work. If you have a car, make sure that you keep it locked and, if possible, protected and hidden somewhere, such as in your garage. Sugar in a tank and things like this can cost you hundreds. (My tires were slashed.)

Tell everyone that he has issued physical threats - the school, the police, his relations as well as yours, friends, and neighbors. His friends' wives should be alerted as well. He might lose a few friends himself when they know what he is doing.

If you do get a protective/restraining order, do not believe that this makes you bullet proof. You still have to keep your wits about you and your eyes open for yourself and your children. Drugs and drink overcome any legal restrictions placed upon the individual.

Please remember the police can't watch your spouse for 24 hours a day. So you are going to have to be ever vigilant to your surroundings. Don't take any chances of going out after dark for a while, at least until feelings have calmed down a bit. Do not travel alone at night. If you work late, have the security guard or a male co-worker walk you to your car. Do not take unnecessary risks. <u>Never</u> get into an empty elevator. You may get a surprise on the next floor if you do - and there will be no witnesses.

If you have taken refuge in a women's shelter/refuge which is hidden from general view, never, ever tell anyone the address of the place. If you do this, then you subject every person in that house to danger.

Think of it this way, if you want to talk to your mother and meet her anywhere, make her keep it a secret and meet her well away from the refuge. Do not tell her the address of your refuge. She can't give it to your spouse if she doesn't know it, and she can't pass it on to your father, who could sympathize with your ex. This applies to sisters and girlfriends, too. The social worker that got you into the refuge has probably told you this, but I can't emphasize it enough. Only those in the shelter should know the address. If your children are older and able to recite an address, impress upon them the importance of the safety of everyone in the house.

You are important! You are bright, clever, and unique. You can do anything you set your mind to. Have belief in yourself and you will find success. Success and happiness are worth every effort. Do not suffer in silence!

I had the cruelest of marriages in every possible way. Mistresses, and being told I was ugly, worthless, and brainless when, in fact, I was none of these things. Now that they are grown, my children see their father for what he is and treat him accordingly. I am now a very happy granny and love my life. I have worked with a number of women on a private basis where violence is concerned and always swore I'd help any woman who needed it, regardless of any consideration of money.

The "Amicable Divorce"

Connie

Most women feel shame about finally deciding to divorce, even many women who have been badly mistreated in their marriage. Shame is an inescapable feeling at this time of insecurity in your life, bringing with it a sense of failure, self-disappointment, and even public embarrassment. (Think of all the well-wishing relatives who gave you all those wedding gifts! What must they be thinking of you now?)

I don't think many people would disagree with me when I say that women are more apt to feel shame than men. Society has programmed us that way. Shame is a very unpleasant feeling, and it is understandable that a woman involved in a divorce will try to escape her feelings of shame.

One way that I hoped to escape these feelings was by having an "amicable divorce." I don't know who invented this phrase. It was probably some gossip columnist dishing dirt on the split-ups of wealthy people. Few women can afford an amicable divorce.

An amicable divorce is going to be friendly, right? That is what "amicable" means, friendly. But, what you'll likely find is that an amicable divorce may be friendly to your husband, not to you.

Before you decide on pursuing an amicable divorce, spend some time thinking about shame, and whether you are being driven by your feelings of shame to pursue a settlement that might be friendlier to your husband than to yourself. Talk with your girlfriends. Spend some time getting a little angry about why society has made it easier for you to feel more shame right now than your husband. Anger is a more productive feeling than shame in your present circumstances.

In 1990, when I decided to divorce my husband of ten years, he had been involved in two affairs. With counseling and patience, we got over the first one. Not the second. When I asked him to leave, he was a professor at a well-known university, a Ph.D. making about $80,000 a year. I was almost finished with my master's degree. A year before the divorce (and well before I learned about his second affair), I had quit my job to attend graduate school full-time. Before I quit my job, he and I had discussed our situation. We decided that losing a year's salary was worth it, because the master's degree would mean an increased salary for me later on.

Then the divorce intervened. To be "amicable," I agreed on a 50-50 split of all our assets (there were no children). I knew that his income potential would always be higher than mine. (Now, ten years later, he makes $175,000 a year and I make $85,000. If I lived 100 more years, that differential will still be there.)

He got a smart lawyer. To be "amicable," I did not.

One evening before the divorce went to court, he visited me and worriedly told me that because I was currently unemployed, and because he and I had agreed to the unemployment, the judge would look favorably if I requested a different split than "50-50." His lawyer was worried that I would pursue a 60-40 split in my favor, or even a 75-25 split.

Guess what? To be "amicable," I did not pursue anything other than a 50-50 split. And that is how it turned out. My husband relied on my "amicability," and the settlement was not friendly to me. It was friendly to him.

I suppose I was spared some measure of shame. I was able to tell my relatives and friends that our divorce was "amicable."

But do you know what? Ten years later, all of those relatives have forgotten about my divorce. Probably few of them would remember whether it was "amicable" or not. I now feel quite a lot of shame for not standing up for myself at that time, for letting his smart female lawyer take advantage of me.

So, think about the future. Think in the long-term. Don't let any current feelings of shame drive you to pursue some ideal notion of an amicable divorce. You may feel more ashamed of yourself later.

You are your own best friend. Work as hard as you can to let the divorce be friendly, amicable, to yourself.

Don't Let Him Talk You Into a Do-It-Yourself Divorce!

Angela Hoy

Eugene wanted to work out the details of our divorce amongst ourselves, a "do-it-yourself divorce" to save money. I fell for the manipulation, believing he really had my, and the children's, best interests at heart. I even fired my attorney at one point after paying him $3,000. (I had to re-hire him later!) The "amicable" divorce decree we drew up was a real mess and, later, another attorney couldn't believe the judge had allowed it to go through. I had obtained a bit of legal advice before I fired my lawyer, so I wasn't completely ignorant of the process. Eugene ended up hiring an attorney but, apparently, only for a consultation. While he kept telling me his attorney was giving him frequent advice, that turned out to be untrue. He didn't pay his attorney's initial retainer, either. (Interestingly, his attorney later mailed me a copy of his unpaid bill, which I, of course, promptly threw away.)

Eugene was getting advice from friends and family...bad advice. One thing I learned during my divorce is that friends and family, even those who have been divorced, can give out really bad legal advice. The do-it-yourself divorce ended up hurting Eugene more than it hurt me. But, there were some mistakes I made as well with regard to the agreement.

One of the biggest mistakes I made on our do-it-yourself divorce was allowing Eugene to claim any of the children as deductions on his tax return (he claimed two, I claimed one, and vice-versa on alternating years). I should have added a stipulation that he could only do so if he was current on his child support. After the divorce, he claimed them on his tax returns even when he owed back child support exceeding $30,000.

Another thing I wish I'd added was that, if he wasn't current in his child support, he was no longer entitled to half-ownership of the house (that was in both our names and that I was still living in with the children). He wasn't paying child support, yet I had to continue making the mortgage payment each month. I stopped making payments two months before the house sold. When the house finally sold, he blackmailed me out of 100% of the profits saying that, if I didn't tell the mortgage company to make the final check payable only to him, he'd not agree to the sale, would not attend the closing, and would let the house go into foreclosure. I didn't want a foreclosure on my credit rating, so I had to agree. So, even though he owed thousands in child support, he ended up pocketing the profits on the sale

> *In my do-it-yourself divorce, I wish I'd stipulated that, if Eugene got behind on child support, I would assume full ownership of the house and that he couldn't claim any of the children on his tax returns.*

of the house. The children got nothing.

His excuse was that I allowed a lien to be placed on the house for construction required after we endured a flood from a tropical storm. I did permit that lien, only after Eugene pocketed some of the insurance money (insurance fraud) instead of paying all of it to the contractor. The contractor later gave me a written statement about what had transpired in case I needed it in court. And, had I not had the extra work performed, the house would not have sold. Or, it would have sold well below a price that enabled us to pay off the mortgage.

Had I added a stipulation that the house ownership would convert to me if he got behind on child support, he would have either paid the child support, or I'd have owned the house. And, the children would have received the profits from the sale of the house, which they deserved. It was their home, too.

Why Hand-Written Agreements Are a Stupid Idea

Andrea Chrysanthou

When my husband first walked out, I sat alone in our brand new house and my initial feelings of loneliness quickly gave way to paranoia over finances. I had always heard that women, after divorce, edge toward impoverishment, while men flourish economically.

I saw a lawyer, who promptly rattled off dozens of steps I would have to take to guarantee my financial security. When I went home, I was so confused I cried and, when my father insisted on intervening, I only half resisted. He called my husband and asked him to meet me on neutral turf so we could draft our own separation agreement. He explained that lawyers would ruin us both and that we should at least try it ourselves to begin with. To my surprise, my husband agreed and, that afternoon, I drove to meet him at a nearby donut shop, pen, paper and calculator in hand.

We sat down and when he offered to buy me coffee, I saw it as a good sign. We split everything down the middle and decided to sell the car and the house and split any earnings or losses equally as well. We also added a visitation schedule for our children and child support provisions. There were very few squabbles and I think we were both relieved when we signed the agreement. I went home thinking that my main money woes were over.

A few weeks later, I called my husband to tell him our builder had asked for some of the money we owed. He informed me that he had changed his mind about the agreement and that he would rather claim bankruptcy than pay anyone. My whole world crumbled. The money, $30,000 worth, was owed mainly to my father and to the builder, a friend of my father's, who did work around our new house without a contract, based on the fact that he respected my father's name and word. Now my whole family would suffer because of my husband's selfishness.

I quickly called a lawyer, who served my husband with a notice of intent to sue and, although I was anxious, I held out some hope that things would turn out. We soon got a letter from his lawyer, which distressed me once again. He was claiming that our agreement was not a binding legal document because it had not been witnessed and, furthermore, that he had been pressured into signing it.

> *I don't know what possessed me to trust a man when he had proven to be untrustworthy so many times.*

My lawyer warned me that the courts could agree with him. The agreement was just a piece of paper in their eyes. It was not witnessed, therefore not legal and not binding. It was only through some serious maneuvering on my lawyer's part that we were able to use that document as a basis for a later agreement that we signed, through our lawyers, in court.

I am still paying legal fees stemming from my efforts to get that agreement accepted by the courts. If only I had sat down with him in front of a mediator or someone else who could have signed the agreement as a witness, I would have been a much happier person. I don't know what possessed me to trust a man when he had proven to be untrustworthy so many times.

When women tell me that they are separating, I give them my regrets, and then I quickly tell them to do everything by the book. Get a good lawyer, and then smile and be civil until they get you a fair settlement. And when I hear women who say they do not have a legal agreement, I cringe and say, "Get one before it's too late. Get everything on paper, legally!"

The whole experience left me shell-shocked but certainly all the wiser. Unfortunately I don't trust people nearly as much as I used to, but I am also more cautious, more aware and more prepared, and I truly believe that has made me a stronger person in my new life. This realization makes it slightly easier when I send off my monthly legal payments.

Don't Negotiate Your Own Settlement!

Jeana Lynde

My marriage had been ugly for well over a year. I was routinely threatened, shouted at, shoved, wrestled to the floor, and called names like "drug addict" (because I drank coffee) or "whore" (for no valid reason at all). Once, Ralph knocked me to my knees in the produce aisle of a grocery store by a kick to my backside because he didn't like a comment I made.

I guess I was in denial about the impending explosion because I had few resources on that frosty morning when I fled my home with my two small children still in their pajamas. I wish I had stashed away a source of emergency funds. I wish I had alerted my friends to the state of my marriage and arranged for a place to stay during a crisis. I wish I had packed a traveling bag and stored it discreetly where it could be grabbed on a moment's notice.

Instead, by the time I had shopped for warm clothes and dressed and fed our children, Ralph had emptied our bank accounts and reported our credit cards stolen. Friends came to my rescue and, within a week, I was able to rent an apartment. I remember being astonished at the realization that Ralph's primary concern in the divorce was money, not his children.

I knew how important financial security was to my husband, who had been raised in poverty. Even though he had mistreated me and forced a divorce I didn't want, I couldn't be a selfish, heartless woman who takes everything the couple has accumulated and leaves her husband destitute. I inventoried every possession and asset, and together we assigned mutually agreed upon dollar amounts to each item. We then divided the items into his-and-hers lists, depending on what was most important to each of us. The difference in the total value of the two lists was less than one hundred dollars.

Since the divorce, Ralph has consistently ranted to anyone who will listen that I "took everything and left him with nothing." The moral here: You won't be given credit for your kindness, and you are likely to be treated badly by the other side, no matter how fair and generous you are, so be warned.

I now know that there are very good reasons why courts tend to give the majority of assets to custodial mothers. She is going to need those assets to raise those kids. I wish I had let the court, far more experienced in these matters than I, assign a settlement instead of

> *I wish I had let the court, far more experienced in these matters than I, assign a settlement instead of arrogantly arranging my own settlement. It was an incredibly serious mistake that ultimately resulted in the loss of custody of my children.*

arrogantly arranging my own settlement. It was an incredibly serious mistake that ultimately resulted in the loss of custody of my children.

I agreed to 50/50 custody of the children, with neither of us paying child support to the other, even though Ralph's salary almost tripled mine. In truth, I agreed to this only because I knew Ralph would fight to his dying breath to avoid having to pay child support, and I was too emotionally traumatized at that time to embark on a custody battle.

Over the next few years, I struggled to support our household, using my perfect credit rating to make up the difference between what we had and what we needed. Still, the children felt mistreated because I couldn't buy the expensive food, clothes, toys, and entertainments they enjoyed at their father's house.

Then, in the recession of 1992, my company downsized and I lost my job. Now I definitely could not support the household without child support. I filed for child support, and Ralph counter-filed for full custody. By this time, I was in a pile of debt and my small, old home was no match for his big, new one. I paid several thousand dollars more in legal fees but still lost custody of my children.

Eventually, I had no choice but to file for bankruptcy to resolve my accumulated debts – debts I wouldn't have had if I had taken full custody of the children in the first place and allowed the court to assign child support as well as an equitable portion of marital assets.

In my experience, a woman's worst enemy, in a divorce action, is her own trust, compassion, love, and integrity. My advice is to take off your gloves. Set aside your emotions for the duration of the court and business proceedings. Find and accept the most powerful advisors you can obtain, and take whatever the court will let you have, both materially and in terms of child custody. You can always grant more assets or visitation time to your former spouse later, if you feel it's fair,

> A woman's worst enemy, in a divorce action, is her own trust, compassion, love, and integrity.

but you must gain control of assets and custody in order to have those options.

This is not the time to be sweet and nice. If you don't look out for your own interests to the very best of your ability during this perilous time, you may regret it for the rest of your life. Be strong. Be tough. Win.

Jeana Lynde is an internationally published freelance writer of dramatic fiction, nonfiction and medical abstracts. In 1995, she gave birth to a fourth child who is currently growing up happily with both parents.

When He Says, "You Don't Need a Lawyer", You Do!

Kelly Kennedy

When I got my divorce, it all seemed very amicable. We talked about remaining best friends. We had just fallen out-of-love. There was no reason to lose our close relationship. And, we could trust each other on financial issues. All the bills were in my name, but I believed my ex-husband when he said he would pay half, and that we didn't need a lawyer.

A year-and-a-half later, I finished my bankruptcy proceedings. My ex-husband is now driving a brand-new truck, using his brand-new computer, playing games on his brand-new video game system, and laughing about his perfect credit. I, of course, never received a cent from him.

I should have seen it coming, but I was trying to believe that I hadn't just wasted 10 years of my life. I was giving it a good spin. I'd spent the past 10 years building up this strong friendship with someone who has always been there for me, sort of.

While we talked about the divorce, we vowed to be kind to each other, to support each other through the divorce, to be "best friends forever." But we had also accumulated $50,000 worth of debt. We had both gone to school. I had graduated. He was still attending after seven years of false starts, so we had huge student-loan payments. He also had a tendency to quit his jobs without telling me, even pretending to go to work as I unknowingly wrote bad checks. I would spend the next month putting groceries on the credit cards. All of the debt was in my name because he had developed bad credit. He had run up a couple of cards into the thousands of dollars and then not made any payments. I don't know why I thought he would treat me any differently during the divorce.

We went to the courthouse together to file the initial paperwork. I asked if we needed a lawyer, if we needed to legally divide our debt. "Don't you trust me?" he replied. "You will always hold a special place in my heart. I'll pay half the bills every month." I'm not sure I believed him, but I was eager to be officially divorced and to get started on a happier life.

Within a week of filing the paperwork, my ex showed up at my apartment. He told me he was lonely. He needed me. Couldn't we just have sex one more time? I never would have expected this of him – he didn't seem at all interested when we were together. I asked him to leave.

I think that was when he began to realize he could use money as a way to try to control me. He would pay me if he could call the shots. He was under no legal obligation to follow through, so he would make a game of it.

About two months later, he found out I was flying out to see a friend from college. "Who is this guy? How come you never mentioned him before? Oh, Kelly, how could you do this to me?" This after, "I don't love you. I never did." Strike two against the payment plan.

Our friendship became a bitter farce. "Meet me for coffee. I'm so sorry I haven't helped you," he'd say, month after month.

"Take over one of the bills legally. Show me I can trust you," I'd say.

He'd reply, "You know I'm broke. I can't afford to help you." That new truck must have wiped him out.

I moved to another state, partially to get away from him. My first day at my new home, someone stole my rented moving trailer with all my belongings. The trailer company's insurance only covered the actual trailer. Now I owed $50,000, was starting from scratch, and was looking for a job. My ex offered to help, didn't follow through, and then moved 15 minutes from my new home.

I didn't give him my new number or new address, but I sent him the address for Sears (so he could pay that bill). They haven't heard from him. Over the past year, he has sent e-mail messages about every three months saying he wants to be supportive, but that he can't handle the way things are. The last one was two weeks ago: "I broke this relationship up. I want to put it back together again. I'm so sorry for the way I've treated you."

I asked him not to contact me again, ever.

The next day, I went to my bankruptcy hearing. After years of building it up, my credit is fully destroyed. I could not handle our full debt load on a single-person income. I wanted a quickie divorce and a good, trusting relationship with my ex-husband. That's not what I got.

Get a lawyer. Divide your debt. I don't know if separating our debt could have saved our friendship, but not doing so destroyed it.

Kelly Kennedy is a freelance journalist based in Denver.

Never, Ever Meet Alone With
Your Estranged Spouse

Jane Thompson

It has been more than twenty years since the "year of horror." And that was only the beginning. The process and the pain lasted far too long because I listened to my ex-husband, rather than my lawyer and trustworthy friends.

I wasn't a total dummy. I thought I was "doing it for the children." He threatened to make them suffer if I didn't "meet" with him, over and over again, if I didn't grant custody of our oldest, if I didn't give him the house, and if I didn't let him take the business I had helped build for over twenty years, conning me into accepting a balloon note so he wouldn't have to liquidate the assets.

The truth is, in order to hurt me, he made our children suffer as much as he could then, and continued until the last one turned eighteen, thirteen years later. No child should have to celebrate turning eighteen because it ends "The War."

Not realizing the aid and protection the court would provide us, I didn't even tell the children, let alone the authorities, when my "ex" almost crushed my windpipe in a fit of rage. I fled the house in the middle of the night. Only when friends finally convinced me to retain a good lawyer was I able to obtain a court order to make him leave so I could return home.

Even though I was terrified of him, my "ex" would talk me into meeting alone with him to "work out terms," saying we would save money on attorney's fees. He would go on for hours, beating me down until I couldn't tell which end was up and would agree to ridiculous terms. Later, anxious to end the pain, I paid no attention when my lawyer shook his head in disapproval at the concessions I had agreed to.

During negotiations, my "ex" made verbal promises, but then acted offended when my lawyer wanted them in writing. "What kind of father do you think I am that I wouldn't support my own children and help them with college?"

53

> *If the man was too cruel and manipulative to live with, why did I think he could be trusted during and after a divorce?*

Too late, I realized he was the kind of father who would make his children scrape and beg for what little money he ever gave them, the kind of father who used money as a lure that might disappear the moment the child reached for it, the kind of father who was always late with child support payments (and skipped them often enough that the system didn't realize how far he had fallen behind), the kind of father who took the house and business, then defaulted on the note long before it ballooned, and the kind of father who would sacrifice the mental health of his own children in order to feed his rage.

Against my lawyer's advice, I let his attorney draw up the papers. He was a "friend" and would "save us money." Later, when I had to call the police to settle a custody issue, the officers couldn't make heads or tails out of the lengthy, cumbersome, obscure document. The police said they could do nothing and advised me to take it to court. In the end, the few provisions agreed upon that were beneficial to me and the children ended up null and void.

Even worse, while I was outside talking with the police officers, my "ex" forced our youngest to scramble over the back fence and run through the neighbor's yard to meet him as he waited in his car on the next block. After my "ex" slinked away from the police, he fled out of town with our seven-year-old, forbidding any contact with me.

While she was gone, it seemed every time I read the newspaper there was a headline such as "Estranged Husband Kills Children and Turns Gun on Self."

I spent the next thirty days and nights wondering if I would ever see my daughter alive again. The strain took its toll on my body and I suffered a serious kidney infection. Later she told me she was afraid she would never see me again, lived in terror every day, and cried herself to sleep every night.

When the court finally ordered him to appear, his lawyer was so disgusted at his manipulation of his own child that he actually assisted in returning her to me, then withdrew from the case.

If the man was too cruel and manipulative to live with, why did I think he could be trusted during and after a divorce? Because when a woman is beaten down for years, "reality" becomes very elusive.

How I wish I had let my lawyer seek the court's protection during the divorce process, and provisions for financial security and freedom from manipulation after it was finalized.

I wish someone had told me:

· As soon as possible, retain a good lawyer, and listen to every suggestion.

· Don't give in to your fears or be ruled by your emotions.

· Find a good friend or counselor who will give you the feedback you need to discern which end is up, as well as support to fight the good fight.

· Don't give in "just to get it over with," because that will only make the pain and injury to you and your children last longer than you can believe possible.

Jane Thompson is a freelance writer whose work appears in collections by Honor Books and Starburst Publishers, and a frequent contributor to Florida Gardening, The Sarasota Herald Tribune and The Christian Communicator.

Parental Kidnappings Happen Every Day

Anonymous

Commonly called *parental kidnapping*, a significant number of child abductions are committed by family members or non-custodial parents. Yet, abductions by non-family members receive more public attention. Contrary to what many think, a parental kidnapping can have a deeply traumatic effect on the child, who suffers the consequences of being uprooted from the home, deprived of the other parent, and possibly spending a life on the run. The emotional abuse doesn't stop there.

Little attention has been focused on the loss experienced by these children or the abandoned parent. Beyond the kidnapping, there is *Alienation Syndrome,* which prevents a future relationship if the separation is long-term and a reunion occurs later.

My children and I were victims of parental kidnapping before protection laws were in effect. The worst part of my case was that I had no papers signed. I didn't even know about parental abduction.

Fortunately, eyes are being opened…slowly. For one thing, states now have reciprocity with other states.

Those pictures in the post office and on milk containers aren't from a family outing in the ordinary sense of the word. When parental kidnapping occurs, life is a nightmare for these children and for the parent left behind.

Kidnapping is not limited to the acts of strangers but can be committed by acquaintances, by romantic partners (as has been increasingly true in recent years) and by parents who are involved in acrimonious custody disputes. Reported in the Juvenile Justice Bulletin by the National Center for Missing and Exploited Children, family kidnapping perpetrators are usually parents (80% of the time). It's rare that a parent kidnaps a child for protection. Usually it is in retaliation against the other parent.

What gives me the qualifications to judge? I was a left behind parent when my husband secreted our children away from the nursery while I was at work. They were ages three, six and nine.

On an evening, more or less a month before the incident, he had again presented an outrageous exhibition of temper in the pulpit (yep, that's right – he was a preacher). He'd shouted and waved his Bible, jumped over the altar and upset a vase of flowers, spilling pink gladiolus and water on the church carpet, all in a rage

> *Parental abduction always happens "to someone else." Unfortunately, most people choose to ignore the possibility.*

against cigarette smokers (none of whom were in the congregation that night).

After the children were put to bed, I told him I wanted a divorce. My comment was born out of frustration with a person who did "holy fuming" while, during the week, he sat at home in his underwear waiting for people to bring food and money to help support him and his family. I felt I'd "served" enough time!

My father died while he and I were estranged. He was 42. I was 15. He had always been the grounding force in the family. My mother had been adrift, directed by him. Enter center stage the minister of the small Pentecostal church we were attending. He did all but move in after my father's death. Worse, my mother, in her void, accepted the situation.

Years later, I learned that my aunt had observed that the man's first interest was in the life insurance money my mother received. This "man of god" (noun intentionally lower case, since I learned he did not serve The God), learned that funds were "tied up." He then moved on to a younger lamb, yours truly.

In my pain and frustration over the loss of my father and shock of accidentally learning I was adopted, I was vulnerable.

This "caregiver" and I didn't date. He took me out a couple of times on a "hamburger basis." Then, he proposed marriage. I accepted. It seemed like a very grown up thing to do. It was, of course, a very bad thing to do. My mother signed for me to marry at the age of 16. That was worse. We were both ripe for manipulative picking.

I didn't learn to what extent this person went to isolate me from others until some 30 years later! I had been "going steady" with a young man in high school. He had gone with me to my father's funeral. His sister was a good friend (and still is). He and I had even discussed marriage after we graduated from high school and he was on his way with his military career. In my willfulness, aided by more exploitation by the preacher, we broke up.

To cement his position in my life, our preacher-man visited the young man's family. He told them that my mother didn't want me to see

> *The potential for a parental kidnapping never, ever crossed my mind.*

him any more and that he (the "pastor") was going to "take care of me." Did he ever, but not in the nurturing, guiding way he implied.

As a minister's wife, I diligently accepted my tasks. They included music, teaching, dinners for visiting evangelists, women's missionary meetings, etc. Eventually, my responsibilities included our three children. They were dressed, fed and at church well ahead of three Sunday meetings and the Wednesday night service. It was five nights a week during the annual revival and daily for two-weeks of Vacation Bible School. Meanwhile, he ranted and raged as I grew into the reality that this wasn't the way life should be. My mother had moved to the East Coast of Florida (our earlier home), so I was "on my own" on Florida's West Coast, alone, completely alone, as it turned out.

To supplement income, and to have some life of my own aside from the church, after almost ten years of marriage, I went to work outside the home. I'd been working for about a year when my life spiraled out of control.

There was no forewarning of the kidnapping. When I went to the childcare facility to gather the children after work, the attendant said their father had picked them up that morning. No alarms – yet. When I went home, however, the house was stripped of the children's toys and clothing. Pots and pans and linens were also missing.

I called the Highway Patrol asking them to stop his car. Of course, even today I would have been at a loss. Custodial papers had not been signed, nor divorce papers for that matter. The potential for a parental kidnapping never, ever crossed my mind.

Parental abduction was featured in the news, of course, but it always happened "to someone else." Most people, including myself, were completely unaware of it. Even today, many people either are not aware of or choose to ignore the possibility.

Hours passed, and I was at a total loss. It was daylight before, in a brief moment of lucidity, I called Mr. Preacher's sister in Virginia. She didn't know the circumstances, but he was there, with our three children.

I spoke with him and tried to get him to bring the children home. There was no reasoning with him. He did let me talk with our eldest son that once. That was the last time I was to talk with him for twenty-four years! It was almost ten years later before I located the "baby."

What I wish I would have known then is precaution. Protect your child/children in every way possible, even from the unexpected. I was totally naïve. Things weren't as open then. Today, there's more awareness. Much more attention needs to be

> *He did let me talk with our eldest son that once. That was the last time I was to talk with him for twenty-four years!*

paid to this issue. All parents should make the protection of their children from any and everyone their responsibility. It may appear paranoid, but even scouts are prepared.

My first piece of advice is a must for all parents. Keep an on-going notebook with pictures (they're very important) and descriptions of your children. It should contain your child's physical description (weight, height, and coloring) and should be updated at least once a year. No one need know your "other reason" for maintaining this record, other than an ongoing child's bio. It can always serve as a nice recollection collection someday. Don't forget to update it, and always know where it is.

Do not assume a person can be trusted because you love that person now. Cover yourself and your children by accepting responsibility "just in case."

If you are considering a divorce, make child custody your number one priority. Have necessary temporary custody papers signed and legalized. Don't wait!

You may not hear the words, "You'll never see your child again!" When are these words an idle threat spoken in anger and frustration, and when are they a warning that a parent intends to abduct his or her child, depriving the child and the other parent of future contact? Don't wait to find out. In the vernacular, CYA (Cover Your Ass) and your child's!

Educate yourself on organizations such as the National Center for Missing and Exploited Children (http://www.missingkids.com) or call their toll-free hotline (1-800-THE-lost or 1-800-843-5678) to learn more about their publications and how to order them, and follow through. The NCMEC has assisted in the recovery of tens of thousands of children. Don't let your child be a statistic!

If you feel your children are not at risk for parental abduction, think again. Get online and surf to: http://www.missingkids.com

Now click on "Search for child photos." Then, click the Search button. The number of missing children, and the stories associated with them are upsetting. Take note of how many are classified as "family abduction." Had the custodial parents of these children suspected they might be abducted, they'd have taken simple and necessary precautions to protect them. Unfortunately, most custodial parents think it will never happen to their children.

Divorce is War! Get Ready!!

Julianna Josephine

My divorce story would make a terrific television "Sunday Night Movie". You know the type. The movies that are so painfully sad that you are moved to tears and then wonder why you chose that as your form of relaxing entertainment.

Before we were married, my husband-to-be was very active in youth sports. He was a good coach and teacher. He possessed a positive attitude that made practices and games fun for the children. I thought he had the potential to be a good father and I admired that quality. However, other people must have seen another side of him because several of them told me not to marry him, including the minister that married us! Too bad I didn't take their warnings seriously. I suppose I was under the unrealistic delusion that "love can conquer all."

A week before the wedding, I was shocked to discover that my fiancé had a volatile temper. He resorted to intimidation and name-calling. I had never seen him exhibit that kind of behavior before, so I rationalized that it was due to pre-wedding jitters. Doesn't everyone get tense and nervous before the wedding? I did consider the fact that I might be making a mistake but felt like the plans had been made and the money had been spent. It was just too late to back out now. In retrospect, the divorce ended up costing a lot more, both emotionally and financially, than canceling wedding plans would have cost.

We were married for five years. In that time, we had two beautiful children and tried to live "the American dream". He had difficulty keeping a job or even making money on the jobs he did keep. I was the primary "breadwinner".

I believe now that these financial struggles caused him to be vulnerable to the cult he joined. He became totally brainwashed. This was not the man I married! He believed that the world was coming to an end and began to devote his life toward preparing for this end. He stockpiled weapons and survival food. He became paranoid and believed that the United States government was conspiring against us. All of his decisions were made on these assumptions. He read every piece of propaganda he could find to support his beliefs.

> *The man I had loved and had children with resorted to unbelievably underhanded tactics.*

His paranoia and sense of urgency increased. It was like walking on eggshells just to be around him. We didn't agree on anything anymore and things were deteriorating rapidly. Then he did the worst thing imaginable.

During one of our many arguments, he threatened to take the children away and never let me see them again. That was it! No mother could tolerate that pain! I knew that I had to leave for my safety and the safety of the children.

I went out of town to visit a close friend. I needed her support and love now more than ever. She listened to me, allowed me to cry and grieve the loss of my marriage, and then offered her help. She called a mutual friend of ours and he notified my brother. Family and friends rallied to my support and helped me develop a plan. I had to get my children out of this dangerous situation! There was no turning back now!

The plan was in place. I would pretend to go to work, circle back and pick up the children from the daycare center, and then go to the shelter.

Packing to leave was tricky. I couldn't pack more than would make a noticeable dent in our possessions at home. I had to be discreet. I packed only a few clothes and a few of the children's favorite toys and books. I didn't realize that I would never have the opportunity to return or I would have taken things that can't be replaced, like the baby albums.

Fleeing my home and my marriage was frightening. It was easily the most courageous thing I've ever done. I was so scared that I didn't even go to the courtroom to get the protective order. My attorney represented me and secured it.

While I was grateful to have a safe place to hide, life in the shelter wasn't easy. There were so many ladies with sad stories of their own. I told the children that we were going on an adventure and staying in a hotel. I tried to remain positive, but it was a difficult situation at best.

My attorney called my husband to inform him that I had the children, was in a safe place, and would not be returning home. He also told him the conditions of the protective order.

From that point on, it was "WAR"! The man I had loved and had children with resorted to unbelievably underhanded tactics. The nicest way to say it is that he fought dirty! To this day, I am disappointed and horrified by his lack of moral responsibility throughout the divorce proceedings.

> *Fleeing my home and my marriage was frightening. It was easily the most courageous thing I've ever done.*

And, while I won the "war", he won several battles along the way, much to my horror and disbelief. It was very offensive to my sense of fairness. He hurt me, my children, my family, and even some of my friends. He was out of control.

The Guardian Ad Litem who took the children to see their father was young and naive. He totally underestimated the danger involved in this situation. However, by the end of that grueling year, he decided to carry a gun to protect himself from my soon-to-be ex-husband.

Many things felt unfair during this year of court dates and visitations but what is saddest is that my ex-husband never got the help he needed. He was never de-sensitized to his brainwashing. He was never able to be a responsible father for our children. That was and still is a loss to everyone concerned. The legal system did not help our family in that respect.

What I Wish I'd Known Then:

- It is more honest and courageous to cancel your wedding than proceed with it just to avoid embarrassment and financial loss. It would have been easier on everyone involved.

- I wish I would have known a way to be supportive of my husband's business ventures without risking my own credit rating.

- I should have never given all of our financial responsibility to my husband. I absolutely should have known better. It was careless and irresponsible of me to leave all of the financial decision-making up to him.

- I wish I'd known to get help for my husband sooner. I didn't realize at the time that he was being brainwashed. We should have gone to marital counseling.

How Other Women Can Avoid My Mistakes:

· Don't succumb to the fairy tale belief that "love can conquer all". If you have problems before marriage, they aren't going to magically disappear after you say, "I do".

· If your loved ones tell you not to marry this man, listen to their reasoning and try to understand why they have concerns. It is easier for them to be objective than you. It is ultimately your decision, but try to make that decision with as much information as possible.

· Don't tolerate any form of abuse. I rationalized that emotional and verbal abuse weren't as bad as physical abuse. Abuse is abuse! It will hurt you and destroy your marriage. Don't make any excuses for your husband that allow for his abusive behavior.

· Materialistic things are not important. I was so grateful to have my children with me that I could easily walk away from everything I owned. Things can be replaced.

· Don't completely trust your Guardian Ad Litem. Guardians Ad Litems are volunteer citizens (or hired professionals) who represent the best interests of the child in court. However, they may not be thoroughly trained in protecting the children during custodial visits.

· Don't take things that are routine divorce procedures personally. I was embarrassed and angry when the Guardian Ad Litem checked my refrigerator to see if I had food for the children. I calmed down only after learning that he was required to do that.

· During this time, before the divorce is final, you cannot take your children across state lines. So don't plan a vacation unless you petition the court for permission. Give your attorney plenty of lead-time to get this done or you may have to cancel your plans at the last minute.

· It is imperative to lean on the support of family and friends! Ask for what you need. Don't try to be "Super Mom" and do it all yourself.

· When things aren't going well or something that you think is grossly unfair has happened, don't call your lawyer to whine. This will cost mega-bucks in legal fees. Vent to your friends or problem solve with your family. Then call your attorney when you have concise and necessary things to say.

Guardian Ad Litems

Angela Hoy

When I took Eugene back to court for unpaid child support, and to request his visitation be changed to supervised visitation, we were given the option of hiring a Guardian Ad Litem. A Guardian Ad Litem is an impartial citizen or professional who interviews the children and all individuals relevant to the pending divorce and/or custody trial. They also perform home inspections. They are then authorized to testify in court on what is in the children's best interests.

The court could have also required us to hire a Guardian Ad Litem. However, this was never represented to us as being a free service, whether voluntary or mandatory. In our town, both parents split the cost of the Guardian Ad Litem and must pay the court directly. The cost at that time was $1500.

During our first hearing on the new pending court action last year, my attorney explained to Eugene (who attended by phone), exactly what a Guardian Ad Litem does. Eugene stated that the children didn't "know there was a problem" so, in his opinion, we didn't need one. The court representative who was acting in the position of a judge replied, "I assure you, the children know there is a problem."

During mediation, I requested one be assigned because it would save the children from the trauma of testifying in court about the neglect they'd suffered when visiting their father. Luckily, things never got that far. But, we thought having a Guardian Ad Litem was an excellent alternative as opposed to the children needing to testify in court.

Child Support, Medical Insurance & Uninsured Medical Expenses

Angela Hoy

Perhaps one of the biggest mistakes I made during my divorce was allowing Eugene to pay ("not pay" is the factual term) child support directly to me. Don't make the same mistake I did! If this book teaches you only one thing, let it be that many people will not do the right thing when it comes to caring for their children!

You must insist child support be deducted (garnished) from your spouse's wages. Do not believe the probable lie that he will make all payments on time and directly to you. For obvious reasons, many states now automatically require wage garnishment for child support payments. If they didn't, many support payments would be late or not paid at all. However, your spouse probably knows that this can be bypassed with a simple legal agreement between the two of you. Don't fall victim to this tactic! I can't stress strongly enough that this is not something you can compromise on. He knows it will take much longer (perhaps years!) to get any support payments from him if his wages aren't garnished.

My ex convinced me that having his wages garnished would be embarrassing, possibly even leading to him getting fired from his job. I, stupidly, believed him. The reality is that most companies already garnish wages from many divorced employees. It's a common and accepted occurrence. While Eugene may have claimed to fear embarrassment, my gullibility only provided him with cash in his pocket that belonged to the children. Over the course of more than four years, he missed more than 90 child support payments (he made less than 10). In the end, he owed more than $30,000 in unpaid child support, insurance, uninsured medical expenses (of which he was responsible for half), and interest.

If your spouse is unreliable and frequently unemployed or underemployed (earning less than his potential), you should also request he reimburse you for medical insurance rather than carrying the children on his policy. (This amount should be added to his child support payments and also garnished from his wages.) Otherwise, you will probably find your children uninsured at some point in the future. Your spouse won't openly admit your children are no longer insured.

You'll simply find out one day when you receive a denial of benefits letter in the mail after a visit to the pediatrician or emergency room. And, getting insurance after a lapse in coverage renders pre-existing conditions uncovered for specific periods and may also make obtaining new insurance very difficult, if not impossible, especially if your child has a condition requiring ongoing medical care.

Eugene was supposed to insure the children. However, whenever he lost his job, the children were left with sporadic periods of no health insurance. If something catastrophic happens and your children are not insured, you can bet the doctors and hospitals are going to beat down your door for payment, not his.

Keep a spreadsheet or print ledger of every child support payment due and, if payment is received, when it was received. On the spreadsheet or ledger, keep a running balance of what is currently due. I was shocked when I did this a year after our divorce and discovered how much money Eugene actually owed after only twelve months.

Keep a separate spreadsheet or ledger detailing all uninsured medical expenses along with payments received from your ex (if any) for these items. As with the previous ledger, keep a current balance running on the amount owed. This balance can also get out of hand if you don't keep an eye on it.

When sending copies of medical bills to your ex for reimbursement, keep copies for yourself and send them to him via certified mail (or priority mail with delivery verification which requires no signature). If he's not paying these bills, you can bet he'll deny receiving them when he gets summoned back to court. And, if your files aren't organized, it will be difficult to pull all those receipts together for your attorney.

Collecting Past Due Child Support

Phyllis Goble

The pursuit of child support has changed greatly over the years. When my marriage failed, the laws were not as helpful as they are today. During the first few years, I was unsuccessful in my pursuit of child support from my ex-husband. Then things started to turn around. New laws were passed to help the custodial parent. State agencies became more actively involved in getting the absent parent to pay up. Tax refunds were applied to unpaid child support payments. But none of this happens without the custodial parent's active involvement. So, get involved. Be the catalyst that propels your quest toward its intended goal.

There are a number of specific things you can do to keep the gears turning, and I will tell you of a few that helped me. One general rule I want you to remember throughout this process is to keep your focus. Right now, the end of this journey may seem so far away that you cannot even visualize it, but the more you concentrate on your goal, the quicker you will reach it.

Don't put off writing that letter, making that phone call, or gathering those documents. When something is needed from you, be forthcoming. It may seem like a bother, but it will allow the process to continue. Don't be the snag that stalls your progress.

Provide as much information about the father as you can so the person serving the court order can identify him. For years, I was told my ex couldn't be found, despite the fact that I'd provided his social security number, last known place of employment, and his home address. He was finally served, but only after I'd written a detailed letter about his then-current living arrangement. In the letter, I wrote that he was living with a young pregnant woman and her child. I also enclosed a recent photo of him. The photo made it impossible for him to deny who he was any longer.

If you qualify for AFDC (Aid for Dependent Children), be sure to apply even if you think you can get by without it. Don't let foolish pride get in your way. When money is coming from government funds that should be coming from the father, you wind up with a very strong government ally that can wield its power across state lines. My three daughters ranged in age from three to eight, and AFDC was my

69

lifeline. They even helped me get a job at a city-run day care center so that my youngest child could be with me during the day while her sisters were at school. The fact that I was receiving financial support through AFDC really got the ball rolling in the right direction.

If there is "another woman" involved, keep in mind that she will be looking out for her own household income with no concern for your children. Indirectly, you will be fighting her as well. She might call you names or worse, but stay your ground. Her perspective will be focused on self-preservation, as yours should be. My ex sought sympathy from me because he was "hearing it from both sides." Years later, the day came when his other woman sought child support from him as well. She went after him with a vengeance, forgetting all about the names she'd called me when I was in her shoes. Funny how perspectives change when one is faced with a new situation.

Don't be afraid to sign that paper. When I was told by the state representative that my children would be given no state aid unless I signed a paper that was, in effect, like signing a warrant for the arrest of their father, at first I refused to do so. After all, this was the man I'd lived with and loved for years, the father of my children. I didn't want him to go to jail. I only wanted him to live up to his responsibilities toward his children. Eventually, I signed and doing so is what made my quest a successful one in the end. Yes, he spent one night in jail. That's what it took to make him realize his responsibility. One night in a jail cell, being treated like a common criminal (which, in the eyes of the law, he was), was a decidedly unpleasant experience for one who had never been there before. One night is usually all it takes (though not always!). Somehow, the money miraculously appeared in his budget for child support.

Speaking of the absent parent's budget (although it should not concern you, perhaps it does), set your soul at ease. Nobody is going to take your ex-husband's last dime, nor leave him homeless and without food. After spending that night in jail, my ex went home and assessed his situation. He put together a financial outline of his income and expenses. Due to his perceived financial situation, the court ordered him to pay a paltry $69 per month to cover his portion of expenses for our three children. Although the amount was laughable, to me it felt like a great victory after having spent years with no help from him at all. His payments were not always on time, but they were fairly constant for the first two years. Then two months went by with no child support payment. A third month went by during which he again spent a night in jail. The fourth month brought a support payment, and things went more smoothly after that.

About three months before my youngest child became an adult, I received a letter from the state agency handling my child support case. Acting on notification from my ex, the letter informed me that, on my daughter's birthday, the support would cease. The man who had never remembered the birthdays of any of his three children knew exactly when the youngest one would no longer qualify as a child support recipient. Ironic, isn't it?

One last thing to remember, it's all about the children. You make sacrifices for your children every day, and you do it gladly because you love them and are responsible for their safety and well-being. You were not alone in bringing them into the world. You should not have to be alone in supporting them.

Professional Child Support Collection Agencies

Angela Hoy

You've probably seen their commercials on television, portraying a weary mother sadly trying to care for her children, obviously in a poor financial state. Then, after giving you their marketing spin, the mother and children suddenly look much happier and much better off financially.

An investigative news show I saw last year profiled a woman who felt deceived by one of these firms. What she didn't realize when hiring them was that they were going to take a percentage of the child support she received from then on, no matter who was responsible for the collection. Shortly thereafter, she obtained a large child support check (several thousand dollars) that was the result of her own efforts (performed before she hired that firm). They took a large percentage of that, even though they did absolutely nothing to collect it.

I found one firm online charging 25%-34%, depending on the amount owed. Of course, the higher the amount owed, the higher the percentage they'll keep of your children's money. If you feel they're taking too much, you'll be disappointed to learn that you can't just terminate their contract and walk away. Due to the nature of their business, they make sure their contracts are very difficult, if not impossible, to terminate.

The ads for child support collection agencies lead you to believe you just have to pick up the phone, give them your ex's name, and then sit back and wait for the checks to start rolling in. The reality is that you'll have to provide a lot more information than just a name, and the information is essentially identical to what you'll provide to the government for their search. The difference is that one service is almost free (the government usually charges 5% or less), while the other usually deducts a substantial amount from all past, current, and future child support.

What do these firms really do? Many professional child support collection agencies advertise that they can collect faster than the state agencies. But, state agencies are doing a much better job with new technologies. And, often, they just need the right information from you to track down the deadbeat parent. While filling out forms is time-consuming, you'll have to do it whether you use the state or a professional collection agency. The forms for the state of Maine took less than 20 minutes to complete. The hardest part was digging out an old photograph (for the police) of my ex. I certainly didn't keep one on the mantle anymore!

A major complaint about professional child support collection agencies is that they step in and take a percentage of payments that are already coming on a regular basis, even though they did nothing to collect those checks. Some have been accused of not attempting to collect past due child support because they can immediately start profiting from what's already coming in. You can read an investigative article about this disturbing practice along with information on a possible class-action lawsuit at:
http://www.fox5dc.com/dynamic/images/stories/investigates/collection.html

There are many government websites available to help with collections. To contact your state agency, see the Federal Office of Child Support Enforcement at: http://www.acf.dhhs.gov/programs/cse

Their mailing address is:
Administration for Children and Families (ACF)
370 L'Enfant Promenade, S.W.
Washington, DC 20201

The ACF handbook includes the basic steps to follow to establish paternity and obtain a support order, as well as links to federal and state parent locator services, and more. Read it online at:
http://www.acf.dhhs.gov/programs/cse/fct/cshdbk.htm

To search for information for your state, see:
http://ocse.acf.hhs.gov/necsrspub/state/index.cfm

More state information can be found online using the state drop-down menu at: http://www.divorcesource.com

My recommendation is that you only resort to hiring a professional child support collection agency if your state has already failed to find and/or start collecting from your ex. You might also find that hiring an attorney may be cheaper and far less restrictive than hiring one of these firms.

Mental Illness, Psychological Abuse & Stalking

Anonymous

I wish I'd known how incompetent the courts would be when confronted with my high-strung ex-husband. He overwhelmed all of us with his incessant suits, false witnesses, and histrionic behavior. An Orthodox Jew, I married a child of Holocaust survivors who was new to Orthodoxy. I had just reached the age of consent/majority in my state, a young but typical Orthodox Jewish bride. Marrying a newcomer to Orthodox Judaism was a completely acceptable thing to do in my circle of friends. I had befriended many survivors and their children while growing up but never knew of the neurotic side of some American-born children of survivors. I know now.

My "ex" soon tired of Jewish rituals and restraints, and brought home food from McDonald's and other non-kosher eateries. He kept company with an array of troubled souls, many who (I eventually discovered) had police or psychiatric records. Within the first year of marriage, my "ex" developed a game in which I became an unwilling pawn. He played "Nazi" and I was the victim. Maus Alive. If I answered a doorbell without looking into the peephole <u>and</u> asking, "Who's there?", <u>and</u> getting a look at the license plate of the visitor's car before opening the door, the "Nazi" slammed the open door on my hands or informed the visitor that he hoped I'd be raped for opening the door to strangers.

Other "Nazi" games included guessing correctly what my "ex" wanted for a specific meal. If I guessed wrong, I went to bed without my own dinner as the smell of his self-prepared and freshly cooked food wafted through the air. If I patted our dog, I was reprimanded for developing the weakness of affection. If I put a freshly washed knife into the drainer blade side up, the "Nazi" loudly hoped I would gash myself. The "Nazi" became infuriated when my parents offered us cash to get through a rough economic time. He forbade me to let them in the house and refused to meet or talk with them ever again.

In short, every conceivable activity became logistically impossible for me. Gaining five pounds meant denial of food. At 5'6" and 120 pounds, the "Nazi" wanted me to stay in "running-to-escape shape." We had to save money for "bribes" in case we needed to hide from persecutors. He stored valuables in heating ducts, false electric outlets, etc.

Devil's Night (the night before Halloween) egg-throwers became "Pogromists" and we were soon the scourge of the neighborhood as the "Nazi" banged on neighbor's doors looking for "Anti Semites." If I irked him somehow, he struck me. Despite police and medical reports, no judge would help me with a protection order. Shrinks hired by each of us further confused the court, as the judge figured that each professional favored the person paying his hourly fee. A court-appointed shrink branded me as the troublemaker since I hadn't figured out how to defuse the situation. Manipulative idiot. I wasn't beating myself or refusing to eat. I was describing a paranoid nut, and the judge missed the significance of the problem.

'The "Nazi" emptied my bank account in retaliation for my higher salary while I was at work one day. "You're humiliating me as a man!" the "Nazi" complained. The "Nazi" had screaming jags that went on for hours, and neighbors asked me how I could live with him. I couldn't, but when I sought the services of the local Jewish court for a divorce, the rabbis told me to make peace with him. "A lot of men holler at their wives. Learn to put up with it or learn to make him happy. And quit your job, because it isn't feminine to make more money than your husband," they admonished me.

Eventually I became so broken in spirit and wallet that I ran to a rabbi's house in the underwear that I'd worn when the "Nazi" threw me out of the house for an infraction I never discerned. In my misery, I hoped a rabbi would finally realize how much I was being tortured. I wanted help to reach a women's shelter but, in front of me, the rabbi called my house and gave the "Nazi" the address for locating me. He caught me before I arrived to safety. I tried to secure a divorce lawyer, but none would accept me as a client. "Judges hate domestic abuse cases. They linger for years," I was told. "Pray that he dies. Somebody will kill him one day."

I contacted CHAIM, the organization for children of Holocaust survivors, seeking help. None available. It is a self-help group. I still hadn't found a lawyer. My guaranteed post-marital poverty now dissuaded them from taking me on, in addition to the distaste they had for domestic abuse cases.

Life was insane, and whenever I confided in a clergyman, relative, or friend how crazily the guy behaved, they figured I was the mentally "off" spouse. He swore to them that he loved me, despite my faults. If anybody questioned him about certain behaviors, they were subsequently harassed in various ways. No one who'd been harassed by the guy would file a complaint; they either wrote him off as the local nut or were too fearful about reprisals.

Finally, I just left the "Nazi" and took an apartment so I could preserve what remained of my mental health. I filed for a civil divorce (thank God it was the dawn of no-fault divorces, and I didn't need any testimony other than my own), and I tried unsuccessfully to get a Jewish divorce.

The police grew tired of answering my calls and repeatedly dragging my "ex" out of the half-entered windows of my apartment at all hours of the day and night.

Finally, I found a lawyer willing to let me repay him over time in exchange for representation. The issue of religiosity became a factor in the courtroom; the "Nazi was distressed at my interpretation of Judaism. The judge therefore took me to task about how I lived my life in modest clothes, a wig, Sabbath observance, and kosher food. Whatever I said, the "Nazi" twisted into convoluted lies. The judge began to doubt my sanity and my religiosity. I was disgusted because the judge had no inkling what Orthodox Jews do as religious Jews, or why.

The "Nazi" presented alleged "rabbis" to censure me (some real, some hired for the occasion, and I doubt they were Jewish, let alone ordained), and the judge had no recourse but to censure me, too. He faulted me for being a bad Jew, a bad wife, a poor citizen, and on and on. "Jewish women aren't women's libbers. Why are you defying your own clergymen?" he asked. The lazy judge couldn't admit the conclusion that the real and fake rabbis were afraid of my "ex-to-be" and concocted stupid arguments to debase my claims for help. It kept his life safe.

I'd already accepted the fact that I could not secure a Jewish divorce. It requires two-sided cooperation and, without it, neither spouse can remarry. Their subsequent children are branded bastards if they remarry without the Jewish divorce. The "Nazi's" alleged rabbis informed my judge that I was mentally unwell and misrepresented Judaism. The judge fell for it. I lost more time, increased my debt in legal fees, and my attorney wavered under the pressure. I insisted that the judge verify the addresses and congregations of the alleged rabbis. Ticked off at my nerve, he refused. Then the "Nazi" changed tactics. He went after anybody who befriended me.

I lost lawyers, friends, and employers over it. Over the years, I lost my cases over confounded judges (our judge was replaced by other individuals for reasons having no bearing on the case), who were swayed by false witnesses, false documents, and lies. The "Nazi" read a story into my face in a public parking lot about how the real Nazis tortured a religious man by hanging him until he was unconscious, reviving him, and hanging him again, repeatedly for days, until they decided to let him die. "That's what I'll do to you," the "Nazi" declared. "I'll give you back your sex life when I'm ready to." He also warned me that he'd throw enough mud on my name to destroy me forever.

It would be years before I obtained a Jewish divorce. He would convene a Jewish court and not show up many times over the years, irritating the rabbis and upsetting me. It cost thousands of dollars in cash, all my property, and as much condescension as the "Nazi" could make public to eventually gain that Jewish divorce status. The rabbis were too afraid to defend me in civil court and the judge gave no credence to my word versus the "Nazi's" word regarding the reality of my invaded privacy.

The court-appointed therapist determined that the "Nazi" was immature rather than violent, so I asked her when the law would require him to grow up. "That's up to the judge," she replied icily. The judge informed me in court that he couldn't legislate someone into "not behaving like a jerk." He was no help at all.

Eventually, I secured a civil and a Jewish divorce. I had debts that would remain for years. After that, the phone became the "Nazi's" weapon of choice almost exclusively. But he had other weapons of intimidation and contact. The court, my lawyers, and I grew especially concerned with the phone harassment he inflicted on me, my friends and my employers, despite several unlisted phone numbers and employment situations that he was able to track down on short notice.

Over the years, we suspected that his unflagging enthusiasm for verbal torture portended a real physical threat, like the ones he described in his untraceable calls and unsigned snail mail typed on various PCs and typewriters, and mailed from all over the map.

My privately hired therapist and his colleagues were convinced that the man suffered from an obsession. "There is only help for the tormented, not the tormentor," the therapist informed me. "They don't want help to resolve their unhealthy fixations."

My dates were harassed by phone and in person and wouldn't go out with me more than once or twice. Nobody I knew could fathom how the "Nazi" knew who my dates were. I kept losing my harassment suits in court, vainly pleading for my civil right to privacy. The slow-to-wise-up judge was discouraged at his inability to control the situation as scores of my acquaintances eventually filed complaints about unsolicited calls and certified mail threatening their welfare. Most of the people I came to know in the years subsequent to my divorce had never met my ex, but he harassed them as well. It stupefied the victims, particularly me, as I lost friends, jobs, despairing lawyers, and a life over the situation. He followed me on shopping trips, to the park, to wherever I went, trying to scare me and whoever was in my company.

Had I known long ago that my ex's goal was simply to isolate me from my peers, I would not have complained about his machinations. Apparently, my complaints stoked his desire to stay in contact with me via the legal system. Each complaint about phone abuse resulted in a new round of calls to my phone number. Then, the "Nazi" learned that he could evade child support, and each time a lawyer tried to recover the missing money, my tires were slashed or a noose appeared on my porch. Other bizarre stuff happened, but you get the idea. I learned to live with call-screening techniques, and to keep the phone off the hook at night. The wee hours were his favorite hours.

He has never hurt me physically since I left him, although his other behaviors alarmed mental health therapists, including court-appointed ones (originally, the court shrink branded me the problematic spouse for my hysteria). Still, the judge took many years to end paternal visitation rights, fearing for the negative influence that father had on his progeny.

Instead of being proactive in helping myself via assertive behavior, I should have just let the harassment continue. I lost my family, many friends, several jobs, and a life over my divorce. The "Nazi" continues to torment his local community and walks the streets a free man. I, on the other hand, became a liability to my peers. I work as a sole proprietor and never give myself a hard time about the goofy calls and mail I receive to this day, many years later. My remaining friends consider me a saint, with remarkable mental health gifts.

In recent years, a program was developed in Washington State called "In Her Shoes." It teaches clergy, lawyers, and judges about the techniques of spousal intimidation and how the red tape of typical divorce procedures harms abused women. I support the effort. As a journalist, I have queried editors about writing feature stories about this innovative program.

Males deeply lacking insight dominated the divorce world I endured. A few females lacking insight worked alongside them. The judges, lawyers, therapists, and mediators had no experience at what it's like to have your religion purposely misconstrued as a tool for robbing your integrity. They didn't know first-hand what it's like to be beaten, deprived of food, bullied in every context of your life, or robbed in your sleep, and then to have your sanity impugned with brazen lies and all the other tools of propaganda. When I needed legal help the most was precisely when the legal system failed me.

You May Be Liable For Your Ex's Debts

Nina Goodrich

"We're outta here," I mumbled to my kids as we drove away from our home for the final time. I knew we were giving up financial security. But, four-year-old Scott and six-month-old Brian deserved so much more from life than living with a father who beat them and sexually abused them.

Entering what seemed like an empty hole of time, my children and I aimed for a life with peace of mind and safety from wickedness. It was worth giving up the house if it meant this man was out of our lives.

Wandering aimlessly along the empty streets of Detroit through the dreary drizzle of rain, and with no family of my own to turn to, I was forced to ask for help from my best friend, Marge, until we found a place to live. I've always been taught to not bother friends with my problems, but this was extreme.

My husband closed our bank account the day after I left him, leaving no funds to operate with. I had a total of $20 in my purse to make it through until I found a job.

Fortunately, an ad in the classifieds listed a businessman seeking clerical help nearby. The going rate was $2.10 an hour. Not bad for the 1970s. Gas was still 30 cents a gallon. This man liked me and led me to an associate who owned a rental house, which he let me rent for $150 a month. The neighborhood was built of single mothers and the working poor. We fit in just fine

"You're giving up a nice home to live like this?!" exclaimed Marge. Disgust showed on her face as she evaluated the situation. It appeared I'd hit the skids by living in such shabby surroundings. She couldn't possibly know what torture my husband dished out mentally and physically. How could she think I actually wanted to live this way?

We had no furniture. In lieu of a crib, I put layers of blankets on the closet floor, tipped a chair on its side to keep baby Brian from crawling out, and made that his bed. Scott and I slept on the hard, cold floor.

The Salvation Army donated a turkey and a few staples to keep us going that first few weeks. Each day I watered down what was left of the gravy and saturated a piece of bread with the liquid to feed Brian, since he had no teeth yet. I couldn't afford formula or baby food.

Already struggling, half starving, and numb from the overwhelming task of taking care of everything on my own (and now with no transportation since my husband took away my car), I considered suicide. If I had a family, this wouldn't be happening. Someone would help me, I reasoned. But, looking into my children's adoring faces, I knew I had to be strong and see this situation through. It had to get better.

Then a letter arrived telling me I owed $35,000 for outstanding loans. Loans? I had no money. I had no credit. What loans? Phone calls started. "Where is our money?" the deep voices demanded, as if I had some idea what they were talking about.

"We are going to garnish your wages!" the threats continued.

My husband had taken out loans, of which I knew nothing, filed bankruptcy, and did not include my name on the bankruptcy documents, leaving me to hold the bag.

My nerves were frazzled and I was panicky. I owed $35,000 to strangers for money and goods I never had. Women's Rights were still in the 'thinking about it' stage. We hadn't gotten down to business yet.

As the threats increased, creditors finally began harassing me at work. I was forced to quit my job, apply for Aid for Dependent Children, and live on $350 a month to protect myself from the financial institutions wanting to take the small amount of money I was earning.

My kids come first, I decided. There is no place for pride in this situation. Prayer took a first place in my day. Somehow, I managed to find little odd jobs paying cash to fill the hole and to supply our personal needs. We also received food stamps.

Being on assistance also allowed eligibility to attend college on grants and to have a sitter for the kids. Eventually, I met a professor who was also an attorney. Out of kindness, this man helped me file bankruptcy and clear what was left of my name. If I knew the husband's debts fell on the ex-wife, I never would have married. I have lived single for 30 years now.

When Dads Choose Money Over Children

Angela Hoy

In Nina's story, she tells how her husband closed their bank accounts when she left him. This makes most moms wonder where he thought his children's next meal would come from? Where would they sleep? The lack of food for the baby was a horrific consequence. Why did he subject his children to this torture?

I've heard stories from many women about men who are so determined to break their wives financially that they force their children go hungry and unsheltered just to punish the wife. Most of us can't fathom subjecting children to such cruel conditions simply as a means of revenge. There should be much harsher consequences in the courts for people who purposely deprive their children of basic human necessities. Doing so is nothing short of criminal neglect.

And, it is true that if your divorce decree does not specifically protect you for debts incurred by your husband, and if he then files for bankruptcy (even after you're divorced), you may be legally liable for his debts. Lucky for me, my ex wanted to add a clause to our decree stating we were both responsible for all past and future debts that were in each person's respective name. So, I took the debt on the credit cards in my name, and he took the debt for the credit cards in his name.

Later he tried, unsuccessfully, to convince a court mediator that I owed him money for charges made to his American Express card prior to the divorce. He also claimed we were only suing him for past-due child support because our business "must be doing bad." At no time, during those negotiations, did he ever mention the children or how they may need the child support. He only threw accusations at me while stating his own demands. It was painfully obvious that his entire speech was all about him, and that he did not have the children's best interests in his agenda.

A few months after our divorce, I lost my job. I had no money and little food in the house. I couldn't afford groceries, but I was too proud to ask for help from my then-boyfriend, Richard (who I later married). We were running so low on food that I only ate the leftovers the children left on their plates each night. Eugene knew I was unemployed, yet he still did not pay his past-due nor ongoing child support. He continued to live with his girlfriend in his rented, $1200 per month waterfront home.

So, it seems that many people withhold payments to punish their spouse, while others can't bear to part with any of their money because they feel their own needs are more important than their children's.

Save Money! Look up "Paralegal" In Your Phone Book!

Lori White

Trying to come up with the money for my divorce seemed futile. Almost every weekend my husband and I argued about money and challenged each other regarding custody of our daughter, and there was a constant degree of tension because I had begun a relationship with another man. I was frustrated and emotionally exhausted, and wondered when (and if) I was ever going to have the finances to give my marriage the closure it needed.

I wanted nothing from my husband - just a divorce to put an official end to a marriage that went dreadfully wrong. We had been best friends for years, but we got married young, and the only reason we married was due to pressure from family because I became pregnant. Somehow I knew, deep down while all the wedding preparations were being planned, that getting married wasn't the right thing to do and that it would not last forever.

A year or so after my husband and I separated, a friend of mine suggested contacting a paralegal, saying it would cost roughly half what an attorney would charge for a divorce. This sounded like a much more affordable alternative, and I began to feel hopeful!

I still felt very intimidated seeking legal services for my divorce. I knew nothing about the divorce process. However, I was drawn to a very plain-looking ad in the phone book and made an appointment promptly. The man on the other end of the phone was very friendly, and I began to feel more comfortable. I did not have any custody arrangements worked out yet so steps to establish that were taken within that week. We were on our way!

Finalizing the divorce was a longer process than I ever anticipated, but I was relieved to discover how much more affordable it was to choose a paralegal over a lawyer. If I'd only known that from the beginning, I would have acted upon it earlier and saved myself a lot of aggravation and worry.

I strongly recommend to any woman who finds divorce too expensive to hire a paralegal instead. The easiest way to find a paralegal in your area is to look in the phone book under "Paralegal".

If You Leave Your Children, You Will Regret It

Louisa

Minnesota winters are bitter and harsh, especially if you were born and raised in the south. But when my father got transferred to Minnesota it was "for the best." I settled into the harsh Minnesota winters and torrid summer heat. But I secretly wished for that California sunshine. I finally got my wish, but with the heaviest price a mother can pay, her children.

Six years ago, I left my husband and two children in Minnesota to pursue a life of fantasy with my first love (I'll call him Johnny) who lived in California. We met in a posh boarding school in the late 70's. Johnny swept me off my feet at our first dance. My 16-year-old dreams shattered when he got kicked out for hanging out with the wrong crowd. But I continued to dream of the day I would reunite with my prince. After I graduated, I searched for him for years. Through my search, I found one of his best friends, who I'll call Mark.

He had gone to our boarding school, too. I called Mark my tall, gentle giant. I quickly decided he would be the next best thing to my fantasy so I successfully pursued him. My pursuit turned into a pregnancy, which turned into a marriage and another pregnancy. I was living the "perfect life." But I got bored and began to search for my one true love, Johnny. I finally found him, five years after graduation, and, without thinking of the consequences, I left everything behind. It wasn't long before my fantasy turned into my nightmare.

Today, my children live across the country. I haven't seen them in two years and they barely know me. The prince, who I gave everything up for, has been living with another woman for the last five years and is drinking himself to death.

I left Mark and my two children, who at the time were both under four, out of pure desperation for a "better life." I was bored with my house, my two kids, and my white picket fence. Instead I wanted excitement and change. I was tired of all the responsibility, financial and otherwise, so I just ran away from it all. But I ran in the wrong direction. I fell "victim" to horrid physical, emotional, and financial abuse by not just my shining prince but by myself as well. By the time I realized what I'd done, it was too late. Mark was remarried and my children were now calling his new wife Mom. I let my ex have

> *If you think you might have a problem with drugs and alcohol, you probably do. Normal people don't think that way.*

everything in order to assuage my own guilt. The cars were repossessed, the house foreclosed on, and the furniture sold.

Everything had been paid for with my trust fund, which is long gone, spent by Mark and Johnny. Johnny, who promised he would make all my dreams come true, turned all my dreams into nightmares. My ex either sold or abandoned what I had left behind. By the time I figured out what he had done, it was too late, and I was too far-gone to fix anything. I was deep into my drug abuse and alcoholism and believed, out of guilt, that everything my ex revealed to me on the telephone was true.

I finally got sober, started to take responsibility for my actions, and began the slow process of cleaning up my side of the street. It took me 30 years to wreck my life and make bad decisions. I couldn't fix everything overnight, but I could do it one day at a time.

First I had to lose my first love, my dreams and my fantasies. In order to stay sober, I had to realize that the man I left everything for was not going to solve my guilt or my problems. For the first time in my life, I had to take control of my life. There would be no shortcuts, no man, no children, and no support.

My family had disowned me during this entire process. No one wanted anything to do with me. I covered my embarrassment and my fear with alcohol and drugs. The more I drank and used, the worse my life was. I vowed that one day, *they would all pay.* My children and I were the only ones who paid in the end.

So what is my advice to those considering going through a divorce? Don't be swept away by promises made by another man who may look better from afar. Get a second opinion.

If you think you might have a problem with drugs and alcohol, you probably do. Normal people don't think that way. Get clean and sober before any major decisions are made regarding your children.

But remember, this is your decision, and you have to come first This may sound selfish, but what is selfish is not thinking of the consequences that will affect everyone. The right decisions are impossible to make while drunk and under the influence. Something as serious as divorce cannot be taken lightly. Love is not the answer, knowledge is. Knowledge from those who have been there! Help is out there, but you need to be willing to find it.

Offering Joint Custody Can Lead to Loss of Custody!

Jeana Lynde

It had been coming for a long time, I knew, and yet I was completely unprepared on the morning that my husband, Ralph, began shouting, "Get out! Just get OUT!"

I knew that tone of voice. It meant danger. In a panic, I swiftly and silently gathered my three-year-old son and five-year-old daughter from their beds, swept up an armful of clothing for them and raced to the car. As my tires squealed on the asphalt, my 15-year-old daughter chased after us, screaming, "Come back!"

I didn't dare stop to pick up my teenager because I knew she would tell her dad where we were. Eleven years later, she still has not forgiven me for taking the smaller children with me on that morning. She has moved out of state and has refused to speak or write to me for several years now.

My husband had been a good father to our three kids, aside from his verbal and emotional abuse of me, but he would rather die, or kill, than pay one cent in child support. Regardless of what any court might order, I believed that I would never see a penny of support from him. I decided I would have to raise and provide for the children entirely myself, or share custody with their father. I also thought shared custody was the fair, compassionate thing to do. I was wrong. It wasn't fair to me, or to the children.

As I had anticipated, my teen wanted to stay with her father full-time, which I allowed. I was afraid that if I tried to force her to change her living situation, she might run away from home or engage in other self-destructive behavior. Key phrase in that last sentence - I was afraid. Knowing what I know now, I wish that I had insisted on custody of my firstborn, and tried to deal with the consequences, rather than just giving in.

As for the two younger children, we agreed to a 50/50 custody agreement; the children lived with each of us on alternating weeks.

The kids loved their father and were also very fearful for his emotional health and happiness. Over the next several years, he used the time he spent with them to exploit both their love and their fear. For the first few years, the children repeatedly asked to live with me full-time, but Daddy told them that he would lose his house if they went to

> *I wish that I had insisted on custody of my firstborn, and tried to deal with the consequences, rather than just giving in.*

live with Mommy, that the judge would make him pay all his money to Mommy. This caused my children to conclude that it was my fault they couldn't live with me full-time. Also, my salary was less than half that of my husband's, and they didn't understand why I couldn't buy them the luxuries their dad could.

Ralph did not tell the truth regarding our marriage and divorce, even though I was truthful, and he did not play fair, even though I did, and he was entirely successful with this strategy. This man sat our preschool age children on his knees and seriously, sorrowfully explained to them that their mother was an alcoholic. (At that time, I was lucky if I had three glasses of wine in a year.) Predictably, the children then told their teachers and daycare providers that Mommy was an alcoholic. In the eyes of many in our community, he became the martyred, mistreated, and abandoned spouse, and I became the selfish, gold-digging black widow.

I thought I was protecting my dignity, rising above the back stabbing gossip, but, looking back, I wish I had defended myself. I wish I had made my side of the story known to everyone who would listen. Later, those entirely untrue rumors would turn up in neighbors' statements about my character, on custody evaluations that were admitted in court. When something is widely believed to be true, the judge will believe it, too, no matter how big a lie it may be.

I fervently wish I had sought full custody of my children immediately, when they were three and five and I had the best chance of being granted full custody. By the time they were eight and ten, the situation was very different. Ralph had been successful in souring the children's attitudes about me, my finances were depleted from trying to support a household alone, and the children resented moving back and forth every week.

In the recession of 1992, my company downsized and I lost the job I had held for several years. Now I could no longer support the household without child support. I filed for child support, and Ralph filed for full custody.

For Ralph, this court action wasn't about keeping the children. It was about keeping the money. At one point, my sobbing son pleaded with me over the phone, "Can't you just stop this [child support action] so Dad will be nice to us again?"

The court did not care what Ralph's motivation was, or that he had brainwashed his children and damaged their relationship with their mother. He had more money and a bigger house, and (now) the kids said they wanted to live with him. Plus, the neighbors (Ralph's neighbors, that is, whom I had never met) were under the impression that I was a party girl. It was a snap decision for the judge.

> *Ralph did not tell the truth regarding our marriage and divorce, even though I was truthful, and he did not play fair, even though I did, and he was entirely successful with this strategy.*

My youngest daughter, who entered kindergarten the year of the divorce, is now a senior in high school. My son is a freshman. Their father is emotionally punitive if they give me information about their school schedules and activities, so they have never notified me of a single school event. Legally, I am entitled to every other weekend and every Wednesday evening with my children, but they are busy with parties and activities, so those visits don't happen.

I could take the issue back to court…and make my children hate me, so I don't. I have never seen my teens dressed up for a dance, never attended a holiday celebration, a choir performance or sporting event, nor met a single date. I don't know their friends, and I barely know them. Worst of all, there is so much they don't know that I would have taught them.

If you love your children and are able to care for them, fight for custody as if you are fighting for their lives, because you are. You're fighting for that part of their lives that rightfully belongs to you.

Jeana Lynde is an internationally published freelance writer of dramatic fiction, nonfiction and medical abstracts.

When Joint Custody Scars Children

JM Friedman

In a few short hours, I'd been able to put behind me all the years of verbal abuse, the suspected infidelities, and the cruelty, and cling to the two or three pleasant moments when he said, "I won't bother calling a lawyer. We'll work it all out between us. Whatever you think is fair ..." No fault divorce. No fault, no blame, no tears.

I was obviously not very smart if I married the guy in the first place, so I bought it. I wrote draft after draft, running them by my lawyer and handing my spouse copies when he came to pick up our daughter for visitation. Unfortunately, we had rapidly deteriorated to a "written communication only" dialogue, as screaming seemed the only other option.

I wanted more than anything to minimize the impact of the divorce on our seven-year-old daughter, whose hysteria when we shared our news broke the biggest part of my heart. I'd keep the house so she wouldn't have to be uprooted. I figured that was a given as I'd paid for it. We'd split the joint property, the cars, and the few investments evenly. Against my lawyer's advice, I asked for no alimony or child support. It was a point of stupid pride that I wanted no one to ever doubt why I'd left. Not for the money. Never. Only for the pain.

So deep in my dream world had I slipped that the legal letter that arrived nearly a year into the process hit me like a brick. No lawyer? He'd hired a top-notch attorney from the city, an old fraternity brother. Suddenly demands were flying faster than I could keep track of them. My lawyer kept me apprised of new developments as I sank into depression. Paperwork and fees mounted as we tried to counter, issue by issue, the demands being thrown at us.

Then the Big One landed. The ex wanted enough cash to buy his own home. If he didn't get it, he'd make me sell the house, leaving me without means to support our child. The next step would be full custody. If I paid up, he'd settle for a joint custody arrangement. I'd already given him his half of the money, but without legal paperwork, it didn't count. I had no more money to give, nothing left to pay more legal fees. He had simply worn me down.

Joint custody. If you haven't been there, it sounds almost idyllic. The ex didn't abuse children, only me. He'd take care of her as best he could during his time with her. But the reality was quite different. Nothing in the agreement had addressed last-minute changes of schedule or unexpected whims that left her standing in the doorway, desolate.

> *These decisions are made in the weakest of moments and last a lifetime.*

There were the hysterical homecomings when she shrieked at me, "Stop making me go there! I hate it!"

Pushed and pulled in too many directions, she became irritable and difficult. She lied, playing one of us against the other. She had no friends. It's difficult for a child to maintain relationships when she's out of state three or four days each week. She missed birthday parties and school events, dances and group "dates" to the movies. She missed growing up. Her weekends were a flurry of car rides and idiocy.

I began to intervene. His Control Freak beat my People Pleaser hands down for a while but, as the child visibly dwindled, I grew horns, and together she and I survived. Eventually he tired of the game and left us alone. She grew, graduated from college, and is in a solid relationship herself. But the scars remain. There's an edge to her voice when she discusses her future and a toughness that makes me sad, but she'll be as okay as I can help her to be. A strong mother (and these things do breed strength in us) can make all the difference.

Could we have made it work? Maybe. Was it right that the court allowed him to move forty miles away and still maintain the joint custodial status? No. Should I have fought harder? Probably. These decisions are made in the weakest of moments and last a lifetime. We can only do what we can do and move on with what's left.

When Daddy Tells Lies About Mommy
(and vice-versa)

Angela Hoy

Parent who fill their children's heads with lies are despicable! My ex did it, and so do many divorcing parents.

I, too, was trying to play "fair" during the divorce. I'd always heard that divorcing parents should not say bad things about the other parent. Unfortunately, nobody tells the gentle parent what to do when the manipulative parent isn't playing fair. They also don't tell you what to say if manipulation, neglect, or abuse are involved.

You absolutely can't stand by and keep your mouth shut if your spouse is lying to your children, your family, or anybody, even the schools. You MUST tell your side of the story, the truth! If you don't, you will regret it.

After my divorce, we moved out of state. I had remarried and was very happy, but my relationship with my eldest son, Mack, was still quite strained. He believed many of the lies his father had told him about me. I, on the other hand, kept my mouth closed, not wanting to scar my son further. I foolishly thought he'd figure out the truth on his own someday and that the years of lies would just disappear from his memory.

Once we arrived at our new home in Massachusetts, I put Mack into therapy to help him work through his anger and to help us grow closer. We had always been very close...until his father starting telling him lies. On meeting alone with his therapist, I was told that I really needed to open up to my son and tell him everything. The therapist advised, "Tell him the truth about your marriage and your ex-husband in a non-judgmental way, as if you're teaching him a history lesson." That was the only way my son was going to learn the truth to counter the damage done by his father's lies. I had already told my children the truth about my infidelities so I didn't have any remaining secrets to share. I only had to give him the facts that I had thus far been protecting him from.

We sat down together, with his therapist, and I told my son everything. I used words of sympathy rather than anger when talking about his father's alcoholism and actions. I took great care (and it was hard, believe me!) to state the facts, not my opinions.

When it was all over, we were both crying and my son hugged me. He finally understood why I'd filed for divorce. I'd spent so much time hiding the dirty parts of our lives from him while he was growing up that he didn't know how bad things

> *Imagine what would have happened to our relationship if I had not gotten that valuable advice from his therapist. It would have continued to sour as he heard more lies from his father while receiving silence from me.*

really were. However, during the divorce, he had started to understand because he was old enough to recognize when his father's behavior was bizarre. And, Mack was at an age where his father's behavior was starting to embarrass him. (Eugene had made a drunken scene at Mack's 6th Grade Orientation.) Once he understood what it was like to be married to an alcoholic, he understood why I had to end it. And, he understood why I had to protect him and his siblings from one more day of living that kind of life.

I used this example with him. "If you were married and your wife was smoking marijuana, drinking too much and driving drunk with your children in the car, couldn't keep a job, couldn't wake up most mornings, neglected your children when you were at work, often smelled bad and even urinated on the floor when she was too drunk to find the bathroom, and had tried and failed at Alcoholics Anonymous, would you stay married?"

His reply was, "Heck no!" When he was able to put himself in my shoes, he completely understood why I filed for divorce. Imagine what would have happened to our relationship if I had not gotten that valuable advice from his therapist. It would have continued to sour as he heard more lies from his father while receiving silence from me. Later, he learned to recognize lies as they were spoken by his father and was able to ignore them.

Some courts order parents to attend classes when they're going through a divorce that teach them how to shield the children from the ongoing emotional and legal battle. Unfortunately, while most parents take these classes, not all of them play by the rules once they know what those rules are. And, the methods the classes teach about shielding the children don't always apply to all families.

When we took Eugene back to court after the last visitation, the judge ordered us (Eugene and I) to attend these classes. I don't think Eugene ever attended his (he lived in another state) as I never received proof that he did. I attended and Richard (my new husband) attended as well. Richard was not ordered to, but did so voluntarily because it was in the children's best interests.

Richard never talked negatively about Eugene in front of the children after the divorce. He realized early on that doing so would only have a negative effect on the children. On the other side of the battle zone, Eugene seemed to never hesitate to make negative comments about Richard. The children always told us about things Eugene said that made them uncomfortable, and we then told them the truth. Now that they expected Eugene to lie, his behavior worked against him and made the children question most of his statements and motives. Eugene told lies to hurt me. Unfortunately, his lies hurt the children far more and played a major part in destroying his relationship with them.

In the class we attended, the instructors provided four hours of training with the basic message being, "Don't talk bad about your ex in front of the kids!" However, I grew more and more frustrated as the class progressed because the classes dealt with people simply disliking their spouses. They kept reminding us, "Remember, you did love this person at one time. There has to be something nice there to talk about to your children. Don't say anything bad about your spouse!"

What the instructors forgot to tell us (until the very end of the class) was that their advice did not apply to cases where abuse or neglect are involved. For example, when our children returned home from visiting Eugene and complained about being locked in a car in a parking lot of a pool hall, how were we supposed to be supportive of Eugene's action? We couldn't say, "Well, I'm sure your father had your best interests at heart." To do so would have completely discounted their fears and anger. You must support your child, emotionally and verbally, when your spouse does something wrong that could bring harm on your child! If Daddy drinks beer and then puts your baby in the car and drives around town, you must state that this was wrong, especially if it was distressing for your child. To disregard the neglectful or abusive actions of your spouse is to disregard your child's distress and fears.

In cases where abuse is involved, it is obvious that you should support your child, their statements, anger, and opinions. Remaining neutral in these situations can actually harm your child emotionally because they then have nobody to support them when they need to talk about their feelings. I spoke at length on this topic to the children's therapists and they stated that a child's concerns and worries require support from the adult they report these concerns to. Otherwise, you will appear to be siding with the abusive/neglectful parent.

See the Facts, Not the Threats

Angela Hoy

Women in abusive relationships often believe every word the abuser says. Eugene had me convinced that he would get custody of the children because I'd had an affair. My lawyer helped me see the big picture.

I was married to a drug-using alcoholic who was prone to unemployment, drunk driving with children in the car, and violent mood swings (documented by police reports). No judge would ever give custody to a man who hid beer cans in the backyard and marijuana in the bathroom cabinet, who often slept past noon, who engaged his wife in high-speed car chases through the neighborhood when he was angry, and who tried to manipulate his children emotionally to make them hate their mother.

Once my attorney showed me the big picture, I was no longer intimidated by Eugene's threats.

The courts aren't really concerned about small details. In fact, when a case actually gets to court, you'll be surprised at the limited amount of information that is actually given as evidence or during testimony.

What has your spouse threatened you with that has frightened you the most? Try to look at the big picture. That's what the courts are going to do.

Custody threats. If you're the primary caregiver to your children, this will carry great weight in court, and your ex knows it.

Financial threats. Is your spouse threatening to "ruin" you financially or threatening poverty for you and your children? No judge will allow you to live in poverty, provided you go all the way in court (don't allow him to manipulate you into unfair financial terms). Your attorney or you should fight for a fair financial settlement. This includes at least half of the marital assets (more if you'll have primary custody) and fair child support payments and terms.

Getting Emotional Support and Information is Easy!

By Mary Boisjolie

Divorce is enlightening. I found out things I never thought I would have any reason to know. There are so many things I wish someone had told me before I got divorced.

I spent 17 years married to a man who only let his true self out in private. Unfortunately, his true self was that of an abuser. Frank never struck me, though many times I thought he was going to. His abuse was emotional and verbal. He was good at it. Like many others, I felt I deserved it. He didn't hit me, so it wasn't abuse. Then, I read an article on emotional abuse. I looked over the signs. Imagine my shock when I answered yes to most of them. How could I have not known?

I got a lawyer. By the way, get a <u>divorce</u> lawyer. Mine was not, but Scott was an old friend and gave me a deal. He did a good job, don't get me wrong, but there was a lot he didn't know about divorce that might have saved me some suffering.

The first step was to write everything down. Scott stressed the importance of having things dated and in writing. I recommend doing this. He also had me write a background. I sat down at a friend's computer and wrote ten pages on what my life had been like while married. The put downs, humiliations, and general neglect were all listed. When I finished, I couldn't believe all I wrote. What was wrong with me? Why did I put up with it for so long? Little did I know the worst was yet to come.

Frank decided to move out. After all, I was "stupid and worthless" and he was sick of me and had never loved me anyway. We told the children. Three weeks later, the children asked, if their father was leaving, why wasn't he gone? I told them I didn't know. A call to Scott told me to give Frank a date. If he was not out by that date, we would get a court order and have him removed. I could do that? I realized there must be other things that I could do. I needed to find what the laws were in my state. With small children, I was unable to go and sit for hours in a library, so I did the next best thing. I turned on my computer.

The Internet is a wonderful thing, if used wisely. There are sites just waiting for you to find them, sites to help you get through a divorce, and guide you every step of the way and even help in finding a lawyer. Go to any search engine, type in divorce, and you'll get more places than you could ever view. I learned to be specific, and use words like "Massachusetts Divorce" or "Child Custody in Massachusetts".

I found http://www.divorcesource.com. What a great site! It has listings for all the states. This enabled me to research how Massachusetts handles divorce. I found out there was a 90-day waiting period after the papers were signed, in case you change your mind.

One of Frank's many threats was that he would take my children away from me. I was "stupid and worthless," so he would get custody. Then, he wanted them split up. We each would take two. I found that, in custody situations, a lot of things were taken into consideration. Among them was the ability of a parent to take care of them. I discovered it was better to keep the children together. Frank couldn't get my children, at least not easily. He wanted the house sold. Back online I went. I found out I could keep the house until the youngest was 18, and then sell it. Another option was to have the house deeded over to me. This was the course I chose to pursue.

I discovered chat rooms and message boards for people experiencing divorce. Many sites have discussion areas where you can ask for help and advice. I recommend observing at first, until you get a feel for the room or board. This way, you can find out if a particular board is right for you. The information you receive from others goes a long way in helping you get through this painful process. I found there were many who had it worse than I did. I had begun to get so wrapped up in my own problems that I failed to realize I wasn't alone. Helping others gave me an opportunity to heal.

I gained knowledge and brought information back to Scott. I found that, sometimes, when he said it couldn't be done, it could be. I was quickly discovering the great art of negotiation.

After a year of separation, we were no closer to divorce than when we started. I recorded every fight, every threat, and every phone call. I wrote of the times Frank would sit in my driveway late at night, the times he vandalized property, and the times he destroyed political signs in the yard because he didn't like them. Frank stopped giving me child support, apparently in the hope that I would lose everything. I managed to keep afloat with creative financing and help from my father and my friends.

As time passed, physical violence started to erupt. Frank would trap me in corners and scream at me. Once, I was forced to lock myself in the bathroom to get away from him. He pounded his fists on the door, screaming. My son was yelling at him to stop. I visited the police station many times to get my complaints on file.

One day, Frank arrived to do his version of visitation, two at a time. To take all four was "inconvenient". The children decided this was going to stop. It was all of them, or none of them. A major fight began. Frank came at me. He must have come to his senses, as he suddenly backed off. He left the house, but not the yard. I called the police. They arrived and convinced him to leave. Options were outlined to me.

I learned about restraining orders. Having to stand before the judge with Frank so close was terrifying. At one point, the clerk had to step forward to block me. Frank actually took a step toward me. I learned there are counselors to help in domestic violence cases. They go into the courtroom with you and stay with you. At no time are you alone during the whole procedure. A clerk stands between you and the accused. I found that the courts frown heavily on domestic violence cases.

Within two weeks, I was back in court in a negotiation session with our lawyers. When we came to an agreement, we would go before the judge and it would be over. Negotiations were not going well. Frank would not agree to anything unless he got money. Frank wanted the house sold. He wanted me to be responsible for the debts. He wanted me to pay for exposing him and for people finding out what he was really like. He wanted, he wanted, he wanted...

I was tired of arguing. I'd had enough. I was not going to be left with all the debt. I had four kids to house. Scott made me leave the room to calm down. I told Scott I was putting a stop to this. If an agreement was not arrived at immediately, I would file charges against Frank for violence against me and neglect of the children. I would use every dated page of the written record I'd been keeping outlining the hell that had been my life. I had nothing left to lose.

We returned to the room. I informed Frank I had evidence and witnesses to his threats, harassment, and stalking. I was filing charges. I was terrified. It was finally over.

I wish I had known then what I know now. I would have prepared myself and asked for help. I now realize the truth in the saying, the more you know the better you are. I continue to write things down. If nothing else, it calms me down. I know it is foolish to try it alone. I know there are people out there who want to help.

Common Patterns in Divorce

Angela Hoy

The odd thing about reading these stories is that I feel many of these women and I have all been married to the same man. It is really odd how the behavior patterns mirror each other. Perhaps you see yourself and your spouse in many of these stories, too. My story mirrored Mary's story, in the previous chapter, more than any other.

My ex threatened to take custody. He was also emotionally and verbally abusive. He, too, refused to move out and I had to obtain a protective order to make him leave.

I also began recording every new event. I even recorded phone calls, including one from my daughter who'd called my office to beg me not to leave her father for my boyfriend. She later told me the phone call was Eugene's idea.

My children, too, screamed at Eugene to stop yelling at me. And, like Mary's ex, Eugene would usually only take one child at a time for visitation, rather than all three. He claimed it was so he could spend more quality time with the children one-on-one. My attorney speculated it was because he either couldn't handle them all together at once, or that he was trying to stop me from going on dates while he had visitation. Either way, the children were hurt greatly by this. They assumed he just didn't want to see them as often. Years later, when we were living in another state, Eugene said he was going to start flying the children to his house one-at-a-time. Rest assured that never happened.

Like Mary, in the beginning, I recorded everything for my attorney. He called it my diary. I had to think back to the day we first met and write everything down to the present. It was incredible to see everything there, in black and white. You could definitely see a pattern emerging in the 50+ pages of small print that told the story of my marriage. To remember things, I pulled out letters and notes I'd written to my spouse over the years, mentioning specific incidents while begging him to stop drinking. I also asked my mother, sister, and friends to help me recall specific incidents.

And, like Mary, I sought help online. Even years later, when we had to take Eugene back to court, I obtained valuable advice online concerning overdue child support and supervised visitation.

The Spiritual Journey Through Divorce

Rev. Sonja Dalglish
Hope Hospice, New Braunfels, Texas

Deciding the right thing to do has always been more difficult than doing it. While deciding whether or not to divorce, I descended into a blackness that became a long, dark valley, both emotionally and spiritually. To this day, I do not know the length of the valley, maybe one year, maybe two. Time had no meaning. And, although I believe that God always answers prayer, when I prayed for God to tell me whether to divorce or stay married, I heard nothing. It was as if the words fell into a well so deep that I could not even hear the splash.

Nice girls don't divorce. Divorce was not an option. Many years before, my great uncle had divorced. His mother declared him dead. When I was nineteen, my great-grandmother was on her deathbed. She called all the relatives to her side, except her son. If you divorced, the family divorced you. Divorce was not an option.

My first marriage was a mistake. I tried for 13 years to make it work. He did not like to hear me talk. I got so used to being interrupted that it took me years to learn how to finish a sentence. He didn't like my singing. I stopped. I was told to stay home and not put miles on the car. He checked the odometer. I was monitored and controlled daily. I changed in order to make him happy. Everything had to be his way. Once, I moved the TV. He put it in the trunk of the car. He brought it back, but it had to be where he wanted it. There were other events so humiliating it is hard to even think about them. I began to judge my life against concentration camp survivors, telling myself if people could survive the camps, then I, too, could survive. My existence was far better than theirs.

I knew marriage could be better than this. For five years, I asked to go to marriage counseling, but he refused. He did not want to hear me say bad things about him to someone else. He called the night before the divorce was to be final and said he was ready for counseling. It was too late. He had told me for thirteen years that he could not change. I finally believed him.

Throughout the marriage, he struggled with anxiety and depression. On Saturdays and Sundays, he got up to eat and then went for a morning and afternoon nap. At about four each day, he rose and sometimes took the kids to the pool. This was also his pattern on vacation. My aunt, who stayed with us for a couple of weeks, asked me how I tolerated it. She thought it was not a marriage. She was right.

One night, he came home as I was feeding the three children. The youngest was three or four. My husband pulled me aside into the laundry room. Smiling a sickening smile, he told me he was late because he had been to see the doctor. He was so depressed that he was thinking about killing the children so they would not have to go through the misery he lived through. Life was miserable. He had been happy only a handful of moments in his life. After he shot the kids, he said, he would have to kill me, too, because it would hurt me to live without them. He made it sound like a kindness. Then, he said, he planned to kill himself. All this, along with many other things in the marriage, I was not to tell anyone.

He had the ability to carry out this fantasy because his father had given him two guns. His grandfather had died from a self-inflicted gunshot wound. Even remembering the guns and his grandfather, I did not think of fleeing. Instead, as the phone rang, I was thinking about how I could help him, and, at the same time, I began a life of fear, constantly watching him.

Our family doctor asked me to come into his office at 8:00 that night. He kept the office open just for me. He repeated what my husband had just told me. All I could think of was my husband's smile and the image of blood on the wall. I told him I knew.

The doctor broke through to me and said the words that changed my life. "If you cannot think of divorce in this case, then you need counseling."

This was the first time the word 'divorce' entered my mind. I sought counseling both from my pastor and from a psychologist. Neither counselor was an immediate help. The first week, my minister only had five minutes for me and said, "Divorce is a sin." During the first two visits with the psychologist, I was crying so hard that my speech was unintelligible. I wrote her letters to try to say what I couldn't say in person.

Now, although it is true that divorce is sin because sin is missing the mark, it was not a helpful thing to say. The following week, he was more helpful, pointing out that all sins, except for blasphemy of the Holy Spirit, can be forgiven. He talked about the scripture where Jesus tells people that they should not divorce, and pointed out that Jesus

Angela Hoy

> Too many times, I think that the church and well meaning clergy have told women to stay in marriages that are bent and twisted and ugly.

said that Moses had given us divorce because of the hardness of our hearts. [Mark 10:1-12 NRSV] This became important.

The third week, my minister told me that, early in his ministerial career, he had counseled people never to divorce, to stay together for the sake of the children. But, he said that after 30 years in ministry, he had seen what happened in many of those cases. In cases where there was mental illness, the children were adversely affected and seemed to grow up twisted. Also, one partner suffered and was not happy. He had decided his counsel to never divorce was wrong. Then he said the second lifesaving sentence that broke into the darkness around me.

"Sonja," he said, "You were created for joy. God does not want you to live in misery."

I have clung to that, not only for myself, but also for others. God made us for joy, not sorrow. Jesus came so that we may have life, and have it abundantly. [John 10:10b] We were created to enjoy life and the world, and our relationships with other people and with God.

With the psychologist, I explored valid reasons to stay married or to divorce. I examined my own thresholds of acceptability. The psychologist told me to listen to my body. My hair was coming out until I had lost about half of it. I started through menopause a decade early. My body was getting noticeably weaker as the stress accentuated my post-Polio symptoms.

The doctors at the post-Polio clinic urged me to decrease my stress. I realized that my body was shutting down, trying to die because divorce was not an option, but death was. For me, death was the only way out of marriage. I realized that I did not want to die and leave my children to be raised by my husband. I chose divorce. My psychologist talked to me about several ways to ask for a divorce, and taught me the most responsible way.

Even after deciding to divorce and following the responsible path, all was not smooth sailing. My husband asked to do things on his timetable. This meant that, from September to December, I had to live as though everything was fine, not mentioning to friends or family what I wanted to do. The divorce papers were ready in October, but my husband asked for more time.

Then, in November, with all three children sick with Chicken Pox, he decided the time was right to tell the children. I asked him to wait until they were well. After all, we had waited since the beginning of September. But, he reminded me that timing was his choice. It had to be now. He was moving out in two weeks. He stood, as the children sat at the table eating their macaroni and cheese, and told them that he had to move out because their mother didn't love him any more. I was divorcing him. The whole scenario seemed cruel. The children erupted into sobbing.

After dinner, I sat in the bathroom with the oldest child as she took her bath. She cried and asked, "How can you do this to me? I deserve a two-parent family." I agreed with her. She did deserve a two-parent family.

For Thanksgiving, I took the child that was still contagious with Chicken Pox to a friend's house. The others went to my husband's parents' house. This, too, seemed cruel to me, to separate the children on a holiday. Then, the weekend before the oldest child's birthday in December, my husband moved out. This was a cruelty to our daughter, but things for me were much better.

On Christmas Day, I sat alone in church. My family celebrated on Christmas Eve; his family celebrated Christmas Day. Even as I sat in the church, thinking that I ought to be sad, I was not. For the first time in many months, I felt God's presence and I felt as if my prayers came back answered, instead of falling into a deep well. I felt as if God's Spirit moved around me, surrounding me, holding me, and telling me that I was loved. I was loved, even though I had chosen to divorce. And I felt a glow of light around me. I was no longer in that dark valley.

Too many times, I think that the church and well meaning clergy have told women to stay in marriages that are bent and twisted and ugly. Shortly after that Christmas, the husband of one of my neighbors killed her three children. Her children had attended preschool with mine. I had tried to reach out and help her, but I was in the midst of my own dark valley. Her husband pulled her children, one by one, into his bedroom and hit them on the head with a hammer. He then burnt the house down around them and himself. She escaped out a bedroom window, but no one could save the others.

Her tragedy made me realize how fortunate I had been. It also reinforced my fear. Don't count on being fortunate. Ensure your safety.

After my divorce, self-recriminations that I had not been a good steward continued to assault my thoughts, falling on me like little arrows. I had known from the first that the marriage would be difficult, but I was sure that God would give me the strength to handle it.

"No testing has overtaken you that is not common to everyone. God is faithful, and he will not let you be tested beyond your strength." [I Corinthians 10:13a]

So, why could I not stay in the marriage and make it work?

My pastor pointed to the rest of the verse, "but with the testing he will also provide the way out so that you may be able to endure it." [I Corinthians 10:13b]

Driving onto a church campground nine months after the divorce, I felt the pinging of the arrows stop. It was as if I had entered a protective dome that shielded me from all accusations. I realized that, with the help of other people of faith, I had tried with everything I had to make the marriage succeed. But a marriage is not one person. It takes two.

Marriage can be a blessing. In a good marriage, the couple can be like the church in miniature, each being Christ to each other, giving love and acceptance not found in the rest of life. A good marriage is built on mutual respect and love. Marriage is for the benefit of everyone in it. If it is not good for one, then it is not a good marriage. It must also be a healthy environment for those around them, especially the children.

Divorce can also be a blessing. Jesus told a group that Moses gave them divorce because of the hardness of their hearts [Mark 10:5], but I have learned to think of that passage in a new and different way. God is a God of relationship, not divorce, but I think that sometimes it is our relationships that grieve God more than any divorce. Of course, God wants to save us from pain, just as we want to protect our children. Divorce is painful, emotionally and spiritually, but it can be the way to a new life. If you need to get out of a marriage, there is a way other than death. God gave it to us through Moses. You don't have to simply endure. That is what I wish I had known a long time ago. And when marrying or divorcing, I wish I had known to ask myself the question, "Can I serve God better married to this person, or single?"

I have struggled with the prayers for guidance that seemed to go unanswered. I now understand God's silence during my darkest days in a couple of ways. First, God would always be with me, whether I divorced or not. Second, when I could not hear that still, small voice of God, God sent a doctor, a pastor, a psychologist, and eventually a lawyer to guide me. Then, a friend appeared to walk with me. Since then, God has richly blessed me with a loving husband, an additional daughter, and meaningful work.

After I divorced, I rededicated my life to God. I remarried and attended seminary as I had been encouraged to do for the previous twenty years. I have raised all four children, teaching them the best I can about love and forgiveness, not only for others, but also for themselves. I am now a Hospice chaplain, walking with others through their dark valleys. I serve people with terminal illnesses and their family and friends, each of whom is precious and loved by the Creator, as are you.

Divorce can be many things. Sometimes it is a blessing.

Rev. Sonja Dalglish has degrees in Physics and Math from the University of Texas. She has also worked as a scientist for the defense industry. She has a Masters of Divinity from Austin Presbyterian Theological Seminary and is an ordained Minister of Word and Sacrament in the Presbyterian Church (USA). She has written one mystery novel, Crown and Anchor, featuring a female minister as a detective, and is presently writing a second novel as well as documenting many of her experiences in Hospice.

Read more about Sonja's novel at:
http://www.booklocker.com/books/466.html

Divorce Takes Awhile, But It Will End Someday

Leticia

I was married at age 23, had my first child at age 25, and was separated from my husband by age 26. Within a span of three short years, my life went from floating on a 'dream come true' cloud to the devastation of being broad sided by an 18-wheeler named 'divorce'. I can say it was a shock but, truthfully, all the classic red flags were there. In fact, they were more like blazing neon signs. When we're young and in love, we tend to turn a blind eye to the warning signs. We choose to make excuses and are extremely optimistic in our outlook on things.

Truly unable to understand, you find yourself asking, "What went wrong?" In my case, many things went wrong.

Joe, an only child raised by an emotionally abusive mother, was never really able to accept love without feeling suspicious of it. There *had* to be something the other person wanted from him. There was no way, in his mind, that he could be worthy of that love. Joe's father worked late hours on a night shift and slept most of the day, so Joe was left to fill in the gap that his father's absence left in his mother's life. Emotionally unstable, he wasn't able to commit to a relationship, any relationship. The warning signs were all there *before* the marriage, but I thought he would be able to handle things. Love would conquer all. It isn't like that in the real world.

I kept my silence, smiled, and accepted a lot of things. Why? Simple; I didn't want to 'rock the boat'. Ironically, what I thought I was avoiding in my silence was actually nipping at my heels, namely the end of my marriage. I went through many emotional trials during the marriage, especially while I was pregnant.

Although Joe insisted the sex of the baby didn't matter, I knew that it did. His mother had convinced him that the first child should always be a boy and, if this one wasn't a boy, Joe was under no obligation to stay in the marriage. She made that very clear. Once the baby was born, and it was a boy, the emotional pressure wasn't relieved. In fact, it got worse. Joe's mother insisted that we name the baby Joe Jr., but I had enough sense to realize her obsession with Joe would then extend to my child. Although we named him Michael, a name we had both decided on even before we were married, Joe's mother still called him Joe Jr. I was shunned at Christmas time when they would all exchange gifts while I sat empty handed, trying to smile and blinking back tears. I was excluded from family pictures. I knew

> *It's funny, sad really how we think we possess 'just the right words' that will make someone suddenly see the light.*

it was nothing personal with me, at least to a certain extent. Joe's mother would have felt the same with any other woman.

Finally I woke up one morning, looked in the mirror, and was horrified at the fact that I didn't recognize the woman staring back at me. Before I had gotten married, I was very independent, creative, and outgoing. I had friends. I was happy. There was lightness in my spirit and the heavy burden of life still hadn't crawled onto my shoulders. Now, I was unsure, depressed, and my self-confidence had withered away. I had stopped working to stay home with the baby (something his mother did not approve of since she wanted to take care of the baby herself) and I was totally dependent on Joe. This had to stop. I needed my life back, not only for myself, but also for the precious little boy I was raising.

Joe and I sat down and discussed things. The end result was that he promised me a rose garden but only delivered weeds. I suppose I really began to come out of the fog when I started finding items in my home that painted a different picture of Joe. While cleaning house one day, I came across a phone bill. I can't put into words what I felt when I saw what was on that bill. There were numbers throughout that I didn't recognize, but all the way at the end was a list of numbers to dating lines. Joe took care of all the finances and I never looked at anything. I trusted him. I dug further. Luckily, Joe never threw anything away. I found copies of deposit slips to bank accounts I'd never seen. Joe was depositing large sums of money into these accounts. We didn't make a whole lot of money so there was only one conclusion. It appeared Joe was stealing from his company. He was an accountant. I sat there on the floor of our bedroom with all of these papers strewn about me, feeling sick to my stomach. I didn't know this man.

As time passed, we grew further apart. The only common bond was the baby. We finally decided to separate when Michael was fourteen months old. Joe moved into his mother's house and, although he was gone, he still paid the bills, except my credit card. Knowing Joe would not continue to pay for things, I had to do something. By divine providence, my dad decided to retire that same year and offered to watch Michael, making it possible for me to return to work and school.

At that time, Joe (probably under the counsel of his mother) decided he was no longer going to pay for anything. During this time, he still had a key to our home. I hadn't changed the locks so he came and went as he pleased, usually while Michael and I were not there. He rarely visited Michael and that made me angry. One day, I finally blew up at him and told him to take responsibility. What kind of a father was he? I wanted to get a reaction out of him. He seemed dead emotionally. I couldn't comprehend that he didn't love us anymore. I still thought we could work things out. It's funny, sad really how we think we possess 'just the right words' that will make someone suddenly see the light. Those words do not exist, at least not any that will come from our mouths.

Well, he finally did do something. Within two weeks, I received a letter from the court of New Jersey. I was being sued for visitation rights. I was in shock. Joe had access to our home any time he pleased! Now he was taking me to court for something I never denied him. It hurt. I was then afraid to leave Michael in Joe's care. I no longer trusted him, and I didn't trust his mother.

Needless to say, I was scared. I needed a lawyer and didn't have any extra money to hire one. There was no one around me that could give me advice. Although my family was supportive, they didn't have a clue either. I searched the phone book and came across an ad for a lawyer that specialized in this type of case. The word 'affordable' caught my eye.

I met with her and explained my situation. She said she'd help me but, for her to lower her prices, I had to do a lot of the legwork. This is the secret to affordable legal counsel, provided you can find an attorney willing to work with you in this way. Although the thought of having someone else running around gathering information and filing is wonderful, the reality is, if you want it affordable you have to sacrifice some time and energy. You have the lawyer as your guide, but you do the legwork. In the end, it's worth it because you always know what's happening in your case, and you don't lose your sense of control.

Child Support

My new lawyer advised me to counter-sue for child support. I went down to the county clerk and filed the long questionnaire. They ask you everything about your finances and his. If you don't know your spouse's information, as I didn't, you only have to give a last known address and the court will send copies of the paperwork to him. All paperwork must be fully disclosed to each party involved. In court, the judge will look at income and expenses, yours and his, and make a decision as to what the child support amount should be.

Visitation

I was very apprehensive about letting Joe take Michael for visits. I couldn't pinpoint the reason why, at least none that would fly in court. (Two words of advice: Be prepared. The judge is impartial and he doesn't really care about the personal details of your marriage. If there was physical abuse, that's one thing, but there is a huge difference between what we feel is emotional abuse and what the court defines as emotional abuse.) Do not hurl accusations in court because it will be perceived by the judge as an empty accusation made by an angry spouse.

Not knowing what to expect, we worked out a schedule. I expressed my concerns about Joe taking Michael and agreed to four weekends of supervised visitation in my home. After the four weeks, Joe would be able to take Michael for day trips and then, after four more weeks, he would be able to take him every other weekend for the entire weekend. I insisted that two conditions be met. Joe would not be allowed to take Michael out of the state unless he had my permission, and he would not be allowed to take Michael to his mother's house. The time was for him and Michael to bond, not for his mother to monopolize the time.

As the time drew near for Joe to take Michael, I became more and more apprehensive. His supervised visits were short and sporadic. In a turn of events, Joe agreed that his taking Michael would not be beneficial to our son because of the life he was leading at the time. Joe would not have been a good example or a safe one for Michael, and it was shocking to hear him admit it.

Child Support - What Happens When They Don't Pay

During this time, Joe rarely visited. We would go months without hearing from him. I don't fully know what the circumstances were in Joe's life that led him to stop paying child support, but I sincerely believe that one of them was his belief that, since he wasn't visiting Michael, he didn't have to pay child support. He was wrong.

My advice to anyone filing for child support would be to do it through the court system. Ask that the state garnish his wages (deduct child support payments from his paychecks which are then remitted to the state, and paid to the custodial parent). If he's unemployed, request that he send his payments directly to the state, not to you. The state will then track his payments (or lack thereof) and can take action if he fails to stay current.

In my case, I had no way of contacting Joe. He was supposed to be paying child support directly. His parents had sold their house and moved away, but he hadn't gone with them. The court tracked him down and he was served with a summons to appear in court. They even issued a warrant for his arrest. He voluntarily turned himself in and agreed to pay. The judge ordered him to pay $50 a week in arrears in addition to ongoing child support payments, and he ordered Joe's wages garnished. To this day, his wages are garnished.

Prompted by friends, I decided to file for divorce. I still wanted to work things out. Stupidly, I thought filing for divorce would give Joe a wake-up call. I called around and couldn't believe what it cost to hire a lawyer. Yes, I was naïve in those things. Finally I found a lawyer who agreed to charge me only half her regular fee, but once again I had to do the legwork. And I must mention, this time around I didn't go for a soft-spoken lawyer. This woman was stern and straightforward. She didn't beat around the bush and didn't take crap from anybody. She was a shark and I loved it. My parents lent me the money for the divorce.

Events took a turn. Joe did finally show up and asked if I would drop the divorce. He didn't want to end the marriage and wanted to work things out. He assured me things were changing in his life. Part of me was screaming "No!" but another part of me believed God would not want me to end the marriage, that he would look down on my selfishness, especially now that there was a chance to work things out. Yes, I realize now how warped my view of God was. I convinced myself that Michael needed a 'dad'. Surely, somewhere down deep inside, I still loved Joe...didn't I? So I agreed to drop the divorce. We started to work things out. We had agreed that Joe wouldn't see Michael until we worked things out between ourselves. I almost believed it would happen. Disappointingly, once again, Joe disappeared and now I had lost the $1500 my parents had lent me for my lawyer.

I'd had enough...finally.

The Move and My 'Final' Divorce

I had finished school. Michael was happy. I was happy. Life was good. My older brother and his wife had decided to move out to Colorado the previous summer and now they really wanted Michael and me to go out there. I didn't want to go at first, but slowly a desire for Colorado began to grow inside me. Before I knew it, I had all my furniture sold and what little I had left was packed into a truck. My younger brother accompanied me for the move (we drove). Off we went to start a new life, all with my parents' blessing. I was determined to go out there, find a great job, and buy a house, all within a year, because I wanted my parents to move out there, too. My dad had become the father figure in Michael's life and they would miss each other terribly.

Miraculously, Joe resurfaced once again. We met and I informed him of the move. I was afraid for a moment that he would fight me for Michael, but thankfully he didn't. Joe expressed to me that he wanted to talk some more and maybe move with us and build a new life...blah, blah, blah. This time around, I nodded and smiled and just moved on. I haven't seen Joe face-to-face since.

Although Joe had not protested my move to Colorado with Michael, I still checked with the court and child support division to make sure there weren't any legal ramifications for me if he decided to change his mind. I didn't want kidnapping charges filed against me. I was told all I had to do was give my new address to the court, and that was it. I left a large paper trail.

I would advise, if you're going to make a move like this (provided your divorce decree or the courts allow it), and if you can't get your spouse's signature of agreement on a document, just type out a letter indicating your intentions with contact information, get it notarized and mail it to all the court contacts you've had dealings with, including the lawyers. Why? This is a trail that will allow any judge to realize your intentions were not to sneak away.

Five years had passed since the separation and I was desperate to end the marriage. I had tried everything to make it work, and I was now ready to let go, physically and spiritually.

> To my utter shock, I found out I didn't need a lawyer to file for divorce!

Here I was again, filing for divorce. I didn't have money, so what could I do now? I shopped around for a lawyer and all were $4,000 and up. I couldn't afford any. I had nightmares that I wouldn't be able to get divorced!

One day, I was sitting at the kitchen table leafing through the phone book and I came across an ad for a paralegal office that specialized in divorce. I decided to give them a call. To my utter shock, I found out I didn't need a lawyer to file for divorce! The paralegal office gave me the package that contained all the paperwork I needed. It was overwhelming when I first looked at all the papers, but the paralegals assured me they would help me fill it out and then, for a small fee, they would file it. Their fee for helping was $125! I was getting divorced!

Since I only had a vague idea of where Joe was, and I did have a last place of residence, I was required by the court to send a certified letter to that address. Even if he didn't respond, even if he didn't live there, as long as I had proof that I had made a 'reasonable effort' to contact him, they would let me file. The paperwork was filed and, within two weeks, I received notice to appear in court for a divorce hearing. I was beyond happy.

Closure

Fighting the unreasonable fear that something would suddenly be wrong in the paperwork and I would have to re-file and wait another six months, I showed up in court. Mine was the last case to be heard that day. I was sworn in. The judge asked me a couple of routine questions like "Do you think counseling would help this marriage?" Hmm. No. I requested to keep my last name because I didn't want to have a different name than Michael.

Within ten minutes, the judge declared the marriage dissolved. I was free. Finally, I could start anew. I walked out of the courtroom, paused, took a deep breath, and smiled like I've never smiled before. Freedom is an incredible feeling that can't be put into words.

Yes, I am willing to love again and share my life. God heals and life is good. Situations arise in our lives that have the potential to destroy us, not so much because they are so powerful, but because we let them. I reminded myself "This too shall pass." And it did.

Great Websites on Divorce

Domestic violence hotlines and resources
http://www.feminist.org/911/crisis.html

Download divorce forms
http://www.mydivorcedocuments.com
All states. Costs range from $29.95 to $49.95.

Or, search for "free divorce kit" and the name of your state in your favorite search engine. You might get lucky and find actual free forms for your state, but probably not. It's worth a try. Many websites that advertise "free divorce forms" don't actually offer them. They're just trying to get you to click on their link and buy from them.

Find an attorney
http://www.attorneyfind.com
http://www.lawyers.com

Find a paralegal
http://www.lawinfo.com/biz/paralegals.html
http://www.paralegals.org/profdir/home.html

Find a therapist
http://www.emindhealth.com
http://www.1-800-therapist.com/index.html

Variety of support
http://www.divorcesource.com
Offers numerous "message centers" (discussion boards) on a variety of divorce-related topics as well as a large collection of articles and resources.

http://www.split-up.com
Includes ability to search case files (by topic or state), case of the week, life issues (the stress, anger, decisions, and questions), legal issues (custody, alimony, property division, the legal process, and laws in your state), financial issues (budgeting, debts, and the home), and more.

Put Your Children First

Carol Hubbard

Your soon-to-be ex-husband may be having an affair (with a person of either sex), be physically or emotionally abusive, or be mentally ill. But how you talk about him to (or in the hearing distance of) your children can leave painful emotional scars if you're not careful. Remember, at one point in time you loved (or lusted after) this guy enough to make one or more babies with him. And to one degree or another, your children may still see him (and need to see him) through a "love lens." What they *don't* need is to be put in the agonizing position of having to choose sides.

We moms can't control what our children's father does (or doesn't do), but we can choose to put the emotional/mental welfare of our kids first. That means leaving them out of the divorce, custody, and child support mess as much as possible, not representing their dad (who contributed one-half of their genetic material) as Mr. First-Class Creep any more than necessary, and giving them only the facts they *really* need. Depending on your situation, you may have to tell your children certain unpleasant facts in order to keep them safe or help them understand why the divorce is necessary. But there's a difference between passing on essential information and telling your kids things simply to make you look good and their father look bad.

Helping our children to continue a loving relationship with their dad (unless their father is truly dangerous or neglectful) and offering whatever extra support and reassurance they need during this time, will help them emerge from the divorce with less permanent damage. Even if your children's father is behaving like a real jerk (provided he's not emotionally or physically dangerous), try to acknowledge that he has a mixture of strengths and weaknesses, good points and bad. Otherwise, the message your children will bury in their hearts is "Dad is an evil, horrible person, so half of me must be that way, too."

You won't be able to prevent all the wounds caused by a divorce, but you can do a lot to minimize the number and severity of the ones your children suffer. So, before you open your mouth to say something about your soon-to-be ex, ask yourself: *Do the children really need to hear this? Will it help them, or will it hurt them?* If you're not sure, don't say it.

When You Have Children, Divorce is Never Ending

Mary Boisjolie

I have been divorced for three years. I am remarried and things are going well, except for one little thing. Someone forgot to mention that it is never really over, not if you have children. The joy of dealing with your ex just keeps on coming. There are school events, sports, graduations, and holidays. It is never ending. But the visits and phone calls aren't the best part. These are small speed bumps in your life. The real fun comes when there is a need to go for modifications to your legal agreement.

From day one, Frank was in contempt. He was supposed to make my car payments. The car was repossessed. We had thirty days, once the papers were signed, to turn things over to each other. I had to sign the vehicles over to him. No problem, I went to my lawyer's office two days after the papers were signed. Frank was supposed to sign the house over to me and pick up any of his remaining belongings. Two months later, he finally signed the house over. His things are still in my house today.

He was supposed to carry the children on his insurance and cover me until I was eligible for my own. Two months later, I took my daughter to the doctor. I discovered that we had no insurance. I called Frank. He said he changed insurance companies. He "didn't notice" they were now only deducting money for a single plan (not a family plan).

Speaking of insurance, uninsured medical bills were supposed to be split between us. I would submit receipts over and over. He always had an excuse. One of my favorites was when he found a guideline that states, in Massachusetts, the parent with physical custody had to pay the first $100.00 per child, per year for uninsured medical expenses. After that, the other parent was to pay half. Frank failed to realize the meaning of the word guideline. He also failed to read his divorce agreement. It stated all uninsured medical expenses. He signed it. He was responsible. After 2½ years, and $800.00 owed to me, I contacted a lawyer and filed contempt charges. Frank paid within three weeks, claiming it was my fault, that I never sent receipts. Apparently, the registered mail containing them (that he signed for) never arrived.

117

Every year, we would have a battle over who claimed the children for taxes. Our agreement read that, unless I made over $15,000.00 a year, he would claim all four. Once I cleared $15,000.00, I would claim two. No mention of which two. The first year, and every year since, I have made over $15,000.00. So I called the IRS. It was my understanding that, as custodial parent, I had to sign papers authorizing Frank to claim any of the children. The IRS agent I spoke to was very nice and extremely helpful. He told me that it was Frank's responsibility to get me the forms in a timely fashion. If he delayed getting them to me, I was to simply claim two children. Under no circumstances was I to let him force me into filing late.

When I asked how it was decided which two to claim, the IRS agent informed me that, unless our agreement stated which two, it was my choice. This information didn't mean, however, that there wasn't a battle every year. Frank wanted whomever I was claiming. Then, he decided that he was entitled to claim the ones who were the most deductible. He needed to "recoup his losses from paying child support". This is the guy who has very liberal visitation but never bothers to see the children. Frank would call once in a great while, usually on a holiday, and take them to a family gathering to show what a great guy he was. On other occasions, when he did take them somewhere, it was never all four. He and his new wife felt the children were too much for them to handle. They were messy and noisy and it was so inconvenient and stressful to have them around.

Three years passed. He would call and scream whenever he didn't get his way. I would hang up. He would call back. I would hang up. Well, you get the picture. This went on and on.

My oldest daughter entered college. As I had recently remarried, we made too much for her to get financial aid. She had to take out student loans. For the past three years, I had been receiving $182.00 a week to support my four children. I now had the expense of college. I knew something had to be done, but I didn't know how to go about it. The lawyer I had during the divorce was ill and overworked. One day, I saw an ad for a female divorce lawyer. I gave her a call. It was the best thing I ever did.

She had contempt papers filed within a month, and I received the back, uninsured medical expenses that were owed me. Then she filed for the child support modification. Frank, of course, contested it.

At this moment, I am a month away from going back to court. My lawyer has told me that I have the right to have Frank's finances checked, especially as the children get older and their expenses go up. Frank should also be paying for half of the college expenses. My guess is, from his contesting the modification, he does not agree.

> *Never let your ex get away with contempt. It isn't fair to anyone, especially your children.*

Since the filing, Frank has called twice and took the children to one family gathering. My opinion is that his lawyer probably told him he better start acting like a father. But that is only my opinion. I would like to think he came to his senses on his own and realized what he is missing. I try to see the good in him. Maybe that is why I am always allowing myself to be hurt.

I wish I hadn't waited so long. I allowed Frank to get away with so much while I continued to follow the agreement. My lawyer cannot believe that I was so patient and followed the agreement in the face of all that thrown at me. I told her I had no reason not to. Unfortunately, Frank didn't feel the same way. I am not sorry I stuck to the agreement. It was the best thing to do, especially given the circumstances. I now have to wait for the outcome of the new court battle. I have put this in the hands of God. I pray his guidance will bring my children the outcome they deserve and he will grant strength to my lawyer and myself to make this happen.

I feel like the old soldier with battle scars giving advice to the new recruits. Stand strong. Get a good lawyer. Never let your ex get away with contempt. It isn't fair to anyone, especially your children. Have a finance check done on your ex every few years. Things change a lot in a year. Most important, if you have children, you need to realize you will probably spend the rest of your life in contact with him. You might also spend a lot of time in court, as a few friends and I found out. We have come to the conclusion that the truth will come out eventually, and the suffering will end. You just need to be patient.

Update

Since telling my story above, we've been back to court. Less than a month after my hysterectomy (the week before the court date), we had a conference. My lawyer and I met with Frank and his lawyer to

> *I also gained something else. I am no longer afraid of him.*

attempt to come to some sort of agreement before we went to court. As soon as my lawyer and I entered the room, his lawyer said that, if she knew my husband was going to be there, she would have let Frank's wife come, too. Obviously, this was going to be a fun meeting. I calmly told her that I couldn't drive. My lawyer informed her that I was less than a month out of surgery. She actually looked sympathetic.

Frank contested everything. I would say something and Frank would start to have a fit. Nothing was fair to him. My lawyer was quietly examining his financial form and said the numbers just didn't look right. Frank stated that he had "averaged out his income for the year." I rolled my eyes. Sometimes I just can't believe how stupid he is. My lawyer demanded his check stubs. He claimed he didn't know that he had to give exact amounts.

Something was up. He knew that it had to be accurate. Bingo. My lawyer asked him about overtime and he exploded. Frank claimed I wasn't entitled to any of his overtime. His lawyer explained that actually, he was right, but the children were. Now, I had been pretty cooperative, but when he pulls the money stuff, I tend to get angry. As is customary in negotiations, I had backed down on a few things I'd originally requested. Finally, after arguing for over an hour, his lawyer said, "Look, she has been compromising. Now you have to as well." Plainly, she was getting a bit sick of him, too.

I didn't get everything I wanted, and I really didn't expect to. But I got what I really went after, an increase in child support, and he was refused when he tried to get them to say that the kids were only entitled to 10% of his overtime.

I also gained something else. I am no longer afraid of him. It took a long time to reach that point, but I can finally say that I am stronger and there is no fear. And I will recheck his finances in a couple of years. I found out that, as long as he is paying child support, I am entitled to this.

All I can say is hold your ground, have a lawyer who will fight for you, be patient, and pray.

Why You Need a Current Will

Geri Sera

As more than fifty percent of marriages end in divorce, we spend a great deal of emotion, frustration, and even money trying to "settle" what is thought and hoped to be the end of a relationship.

The legal battles and wars fought over property, finances, child, and pet custody take priority initially. Then, as time advances, each party in a divorce action revisits many aspects of the settlement agreement as spousal circumstances change, children age, and situations evolve.

One aspect of divorce that is seldom, if ever, addressed is the need for each party to prepare a Will, and that the conditions and expectations of each should be provided to the divorced spouse if child custody is included in the divorce decree.

Dennis and Geri had been married for 28 years and their relationship ended rather suddenly, leaving mixed feelings among family members and siblings. Most of the children were adults, but one son was mentally disabled and dependent on government funding for Day Programs and group home support.

The couple had prepared Wills when their children were young. It was done at about the same time the couple recognized the need for life insurance. As has been customary and traditional, the largest insurance policy was purchased for Dennis and a lesser policy was put in place for Geri. The policies reflected what the couple believed would shadow their financial roles within the family infrastructure.

Some years later, Dennis began to suffer some health problems, and Geri expanded her responsibilities to include employment. She became the primary wage earner. As that role continued, the couple decided it would be best for Geri's insurance policy to be amended to better represent her financial role in the family.

The couple's Wills were drawn up by a family friend/lawyer. The traditional clauses were prepared, identifying each spouse in the alternate spouse's Will as executor. The funds arising from an untimely death were to be directed to the surviving spouse with disbursement options for the children, as the surviving spouse determined appropriate.

As the family evolved and circumstances changed, the Wills were never changed to reflect "guardianship" of the children should both parents die. Nor were there amendments to allow the couple's adult children a role in the care and financial concerns for their younger siblings.

If the couple had not come to the divorce court so many years later, perhaps the lack of attention to updating Wills might not have become an issue. But, shortly after the divorce, Geri realized the need for a new Will and had one prepared. In it, she assigned gifts to a number of non-profit organizations, and she set up a trust for her disabled son. Geri also set aside some limited funds for her grandchildren. She assigned Trustees to the Trust after seeking consent and participation from family members. She also made changes to her life insurance policy.

Within three years of the divorce, Dennis passed away unexpectedly, having left his original Will without legal/notarized changes. He had scribbled a few alterations, but his hand written changes were not understood or recognized by the court. And, they had not been witnessed (which might have brought clarification) by anyone outside the family. His lack of foresight also moved him to discontinue his life insurance policy.

Because the family was fractured by the divorce, one of Geri's adult children found exception to the interpretation of the Will. No conversations or communications could bring reason to reign and, eventually, three lawyers and the courts took control of his estate. All the siblings and Geri agreed that the remaining funds would be placed in a trust for the handicapped adult child.

One would think that after all the efforts to settle the estate, including court involvement, the trust fund would have been established and all would have gone well. But, nothing could be further from fact. One of the lawyers, hired by the "unhappy" child, *still* holds the funds. While the court ordered the funds to be directed into a trust, and the court ordered government involvement in disbursing funds from the trust on behalf of the dependent adult, the court did not enforce the order.

And, the story is not over yet. The family is still striving to have the estate disbursed to the trust. Meanwhile, the disabled adult and all concerned with his care and management are tied to the bureaucracy of the court assigned trustee. The trustee's involvement is only managing the government funding sources. This responsibility had previously been handled, with fewer "strings" attached, by a family designated guardian. The disabled adult's lifestyle has been negatively impacted. Simple expenditures to allow for lifestyle considerations must now be negotiated and approved by the Trustee. The court's plan had allowed for revenues generated from interest or investment growth to be spent, under the joint agreement of the guardian and the Trustee. If the money had been moved from the hands of the lawyer and into the trust, the dependent adult's finances would have allowed for travel, purchases, and endless negotiated options, including eventual disbursement when the disabled recipient passed on. Lawyers have enjoyed the only financial benefits from the estate and they may yet make even more money before funds are legally disbursed.

When couples divorce, the immediate concerns are important, but long range planning should include the creation of Wills or the amendment of Wills to reflect the best interests of all parties. Anger, resentment, hurt, pain, frustration, and retaliation are often the most provocative and apparent emotions during and after divorce. This environment does not breed the creation of positive and careful planning for an "unknown" future.

One sure event in everyone's future is death. Questions should be considered, such as:

· If one were to die suddenly, where do they want to be buried?

· How are funeral and burial costs to be met?

· Who is responsible for the funeral?

These can be especially troublesome when an adult dies having had more than one spouse and children from multiple relationships. But even if there are no children, and no new spouses involved, the same questions pose considerable pondering and decisions may create ill feelings.

When a Will has not been amended and the document still assigns executor roles to the divorced partner, imagine the possible impact, not only on the remaining party, but on the extended family as well. If life insurance disbursements have not been changed, the disbursement of funds may be viewed as "lottery winnings" for the remaining ex-spouse

> *Any young adult with children who does not have a Living Will is inviting unwanted court action for placement of children in the event of a severe accident or critical health crisis.*

rather than as consequences of procrastinated action on the part of the deceased.

Similar and even greater distress may arise if the remaining spouse has remarried. When funds are directed to one of the partners in the new marriage, extended family of the deceased may see the disbursement of insurance revenues into the new marriage as obscene and immoral. If the new marriage has been blessed with children, greater confusion and emotion result. Should the "couple" be allowed to spend the insurance and estate funds indiscriminately? Should the funds simply be put in trust for the deceased's children and eventual grandchildren? Maybe the funds should be re-directed to another family member or to charity? The possible perspectives of all concerned and the bad feelings that develop can be insurmountable and devastating.

One 60-year-old gentleman had suffered four heart attacks. He had married four times and had two children (each adults) with whom he has very limited contact. He had ongoing relationships, from a distance, with siblings, but when asked by one of his brothers, "Where do you want to be buried?" he answered in frustration, "I don't know. Just throw me in a ditch!"

The scenario may seem bizarre, but is true. He is not concerned for his family as they contemplate their future responsibility to him. His lack of planning, minus both insurance and a Will, will probably leave his siblings struggling with decisions and costs.

What kind of people "plan" for their ultimate future? One group of "planners" are spouses who leave the divorce table with "considerable" assets. They file their divorce decree and quickly make appointments with their lawyers, accountants, and financial planners/investment brokers. Planning or revising their Will is prioritized to make changes relative to previous spousal rights and privileges, or eventual disbursement of assets.

The same is not consistent when litigants do not have an "established" lifestyle or a host of assets and investments. They may not even think of revising their Wills or insurance policies. Often, couples don't see themselves as "having enough" to bother preparing a Will. Further, too many don't have life insurance. But, as illustrated by the previous examples and other real life stories, the pain and frustration brought about by not completing such plans is never less than profound.

Living Wills

Leaving a marriage assumes leaving a spouse that one has come to trust and believe will always keep the other's best interests at heart. Just as preparing a Last Will and Testament to ensure our estate and family are given every consideration, all adults, especially a single adult, should prepare a Living Will.

If an adult becomes incapacitated, unable to meet her/her own needs, a Living Will offers the structure and perspective necessary for decision-making. It also provides the framework or foundation for court involvement if injuries or a health crisis mean long-term or permanent disability or the removal of life support, if necessary. Too many people fight in the media or the courts for a "death with dignity". Too few actually plan for such possibilities.

Any young adult with children who does not have a Living Will is inviting unwanted court action for placement of children in the event of a severe accident or critical health crisis. Not only that, if long term "care" is necessary, a Living Will should outline financial resources, guardianship alternates, and everything else necessary to meet the children's needs.

The media reports endless scenarios of seriously ill adults struggling to have their "rights" recognized. A carefully prepared Living Will ensures one's wishes are met and one's obligations are taken care of. It is vitally important to review the guidelines in developing a Living Will and the limitations for such documents. Interpretation of a Living Will varies from jurisdiction to jurisdiction. To ensure the best possible outcome, the planner should identify a personal representative, a friend or a family member who has detailed/written evidence outlining the wishes of the individual in question.

The best defense in long term planning is a good offense.

Geri Sera is the author of The Banks and You, A Survival Manual. She can be contacted via email at: gerisera@telus.net

"Us Children"

by Alexandra Hoy (age 12)

Divorce may be the best thing you can do for us. We will forgive you if we think you're wrong, but thank you when we know you're right.

I am going to have a better life.

Very good people who make other lives wonderful are people like you!

Ordinarily, we love our parents and trust their decisions.

Reactions from this might be crying or anger, but we will soon know the reason why and that anger will be turned to happiness.

Cases like these are resolved and will tilt toward the happier part of life.

Every one of us is going to thank you when we grow up. We will love you even more than before!

One night, when my mom wasn't sleeping with my father anymore, she was sleeping with me. I heard a thick-tongued sentence say, "Come on, Angie. Just sign the papers." He was drunk.
   My mom was like, "Sshh! You'll wake her."
   I was already awake. She then got up and left the room. My father passed and I said, "What's going on?"
   He just said, "Nothing. Go back to bed."

I remember how every night my mom and dad would go in the other room and talk for about three hours. I never knew what it was about. I thought they were talking about our vacation. I just figured, "Come on. Let's go! I've been waiting for vacation all year!" But they were talking about divorce.

As soon as I heard the horrifying word DIVORCE come out, tears flooded my face. I didn't know why or how this could happen. All I knew was the divorce word. Later, there were flashing lights.
"You're drunk!"
"No I'm not!"
Police cars were in our driveway.
I then started crying. I asked, "Can I go tell Grandma?" She was living with us at the time. "Please, she should know." I said. My father said, "Okay, go."
I ran. When the words "Mommy and Daddy are getting a divorce" slipped out of my mouth, my throat tightened. My eyes became blurry. My heart sank.

I later came to know the "real" dad. I remember one night in particular. My dad ran after my mom after forcing her out of the house and not letting her take us. We soon got into the car and drove after her. My big brother was saying, "Won't that hurt the truck?" My dad had popped my mom's tire with a screwdriver and the tire came off the truck when she was driving. We were soon at the police station and the police made my father go inside with them. We were outside with my mom, drinking a soda and waiting.
Also, another night I remember following my mom and dad around listening to my dad yell the words, "Get out! Get out!" over and over. The words hurt, but what could I do? Risk the smack of my father's hand when he was drinking after I said "Shut up!" to him?
I was then looking at my father who was looking at a locked white door, trying to find a way in. He was then running outside to find the sliding glass door. I was following him. Now I was not able to get with my mom because I was behind my dad. He then got in after my brother opened the glass door for him. When he started yelling yet again, she fled to her mother's house.
Another day, I was at the YMCA and my brother said, when he and my mom came, to hurry. We had a visit to a hotel cause the judge said my dad had to leave the house. The next day, we came home to a trashed house, dresser drawers pulled out, bed gone, and lots more stuff gone.

Today, all is well, but the visits to him put me in therapy with people I didn't know. But now I feel as sweet as a new spring morning. My step-dad soon adopted us and we are all a big happy family now.

The End

Angela Hoy

It took almost two years for this book to progress from idea to print. During the writing process, we decided to take my ex, Eugene, back to court. The book was put on hold in order to include advice on post-divorce litigation. The process was quite intriguing and, in many ways, mirrored the actual divorce.

In July of that year, the children visited Eugene for four days while Richard and I went to Las Vegas for the honeymoon we'd never had. Things started badly before we even got on the plane to Vegas. In the airport terminal, my cell phone rang. It was Alexandra, calling to tell me that Eugene had picked them up from the airport (after not seeing them for several months), stopped at the store for candy, drove them to his house, and then, while it was still daylight, left them in front of the television and promptly went to bed. I was shocked. How can you take a nap when your children, whom you haven't seen in months, come to visit? He claimed he was sick. Later, he claimed he had a toothache. Neither of these things (if they were even true, and I suspected they were not) were valid excuses for his actions over those four days.

The next morning, the children couldn't wake Eugene up. He'd promised to take them to the beach that day. Richard and I were in Las Vegas by then and answered dozens of calls on our cell phones from Alexandra, who was not only angry, but also hurt by Eugene's neglect. He claimed, when they tried to get him up, that he didn't feel good. I recognized this as the same behavior he'd exhibited repeatedly during our marriage. Hangovers lead to late mornings. And, while I wasn't sure he had a hangover, I was sure that his neglect was angering and hurting our three children.

Alexandra was worried because she felt she needed to feed her brothers breakfast and lunch, and all she could find was some old chicken and the candy Eugene had bought for them the day before. Eugene finally got up late that afternoon and took them to the beach. However, they arrived so late that the waterslides, which he'd promised they'd go on, were closed. The children were disappointed once again as he had, once again, broken a promise.

Robert stated that Eugene had promised to buy him a new game to make up for sleeping all day. Eugene later insisted he only promised to "play" a game with Robert. That broken promise infuriated Robert so much that he still talks about it on occasion.

One of the things Eugene did during that visit was to leave the children at his mother's house the following evening, after promising not to do so. The children flew down there to visit him and they wanted to spend time with <u>him</u>. They did not want him to leave them elsewhere. (On a prior visit, Eugene had gone out on a date one night, leaving the children with relatives. That angered and hurt them.) He returned several hours later. Our oldest thought he was drunk. The children told us he then put them in the car and drove them to the dark parking lot of a pool hall in Houston, Texas. It was approximately 10:00 p.m. He then left them in the locked car while he went inside to "pay someone money" that he owed. (He later claimed someone owed <u>him</u> money, as if that minor detail made his actions acceptable.) The children were frightened and quite shaken by the incident and, when I heard what Eugene did, I was mortified! What kind of parent would do something so irresponsible?

The next day, they had a family party at Eugene's house. The cousins came to visit and the children seemed happy. However, they said Eugene yelled at them in front of his girlfriend when they were playing. Alexandra was angry because she thought he was showing off for his girlfriend by yelling at them. That night, the children said Eugene stayed up all night long and that he left them alone to go next door to visit his neighbor after they went to bed.

When Alexandra woke up the next morning, she found Eugene sitting alone in a room "full of smoke." She called us at about 8:00 a.m. to say she thought her father was drunk. He got on the phone with me and he was slurring his words terribly. I called his mother because she was much closer to his house than we were, and told her I thought Eugene was drunk. She asked no questions and agreed to drive there quickly. She later denied there was anything wrong with him. What was odd was that I only had to say "I think he's drunk" and she seemed to know exactly what I was implying, that the children were not being cared for. She didn't ask any questions. She just said, "I'm on my way!" Later, she did feel the need to protect him (Eugene is her son, after all), and I understood her reluctance to admit that he was not alert and sober.

Eugene later claimed he was on medication for his toothache. If he was, I believe he took too much of it, or that he mixed it with alcohol. During our marriage, I watched Eugene take too much medication after a dental procedure and also mix it with alcohol. After he returned home on that day, drunk and on those drugs, he was drooling profusely, incoherent, and, once he finally fell asleep, I had to keep checking to see if he was breathing.

After talking to his mother, I called Alexandra back and told her, Mack and Robert to not get in a car with Eugene under any circumstances. He had talked to me on the phone and, with a heavy slur in his pronunciation, was saying odd, irrational things about when we were leaving town. I was terrified that he would try to do something stupid.

Richard and I had flown in from Las Vegas the night before and were staying at my mother's house. After the last phone call, Richard and I got in the car and raced to Eugene's house, 45 minutes away. I was looking for police cars on the way so one could accompany us to his house. I didn't see any, so Richard came inside with me. I hoped Eugene would act rationally as he usually tried to appear civil in Richard's presence.

When we arrived, I helped the children pack their things. Eugene was behind the house. He was crying, actually howling, in front of the children, which frightened them. We couldn't get the children away from that situation fast enough.

Earlier visitations had included reports of Eugene drinking in front of the children (in violation of court order) and driving with them in the car while he drank. Eugene claims it was non-alcoholic beer. However, the children have been able to recognize Budweiser® and Busch® cans, and have been reading since kindergarten, so his excuse didn't fly, and only angered the children. They felt he was accusing them of lying.

They even claimed he told them, while he was drinking and driving, that he was not an alcoholic. "Don't you worry about your old dad," they claim he said. If it was non-alcoholic beer, why would he say that to them? Logically, he would have simply told the children there was no alcohol. But, he didn't deny it until months later when we took him back to court.

Alexandra came home from one visit with a huge gash in the bottom of her foot. It was wrapped in filthy tape and had dirt embedded in it. I believe she needed stitches for that, but he never took her to the doctor.

Alexandra and Robert both had one health concern during a visit that Eugene completely ignored, despite the instructions I gave him when dropping them off.

I could go on and on. But, that last visit was the catalyst that delayed the publication of this book.

On arriving back in Bangor, I immediately put the children in counseling to deal with the feelings they were experiencing. They were angry and depressed and talked continually about what had happened during their visit. Richard and I then hired a large law firm to represent the children. What I wanted was for Eugene to have supervised visitation only (because of the neglect, and because he'd already violated court orders to not drink when the children were in his care). We also learned, through a simple Internet search that cost $3.60, that Eugene had been arrested for Driving While Intoxicated (DWI) twice in the previous 12 months. It was no longer my word (and the children's words) against his regarding his problems with drinking and driving. (You can sometimes find criminal convictions online for free. Try the Public Record Locator at: http://www.searchsystems.net)

The other issue I addressed was the thousands in child support, insurance, and uninsured medical expenses he owed. Somewhere along the way, he'd decided he just wasn't going to pay child support. However, that was secondary to the request for supervised visitation. I could no longer allow the children to be alone with him as he put them in physical and psychology danger whenever they stayed at his house.

I talked to his father during that time and learned that Eugene told him he was current on his child support. We had to assume he'd told his entire family the same thing. So, we knew that, in his family's eyes, I was still the villain. And, we had to assume that these lies would eventually flow down the family tree to the children.

While the legal wrangling got under way, Eugene spent 30 days in jail for his second DWI. He told us he was in Peru at the time (he lied to us and to the children). He then really did go to Peru and was there, unemployed by choice, until January of the following year. I spoke to his mother a few times while he was gone. She seemed fed up with needing to send him money while he was off "finding himself." She also told me that he was robbed at an ATM machine while there which required a trip to the hospital for his injuries.

That brought back memories of one night, early in our marriage, when Eugene came home, beat up, claiming he was late because he was attacked in the parking lot of a bar. Years later, he admitted he'd punched himself and made up the story as an excuse to be late so I wouldn't be angry. On hearing his mother's comments, I was thankful that I no longer had to deal with Eugene's continuing problems.

One concern that was looming in my mind was what would happen to the children if something happened to me. I thought that Eugene might swoop in, at the time of my death, and take custody of the children while requesting funds from our business, which I co-owned, to care for them. He could then be financially secure and not need to get a job, and might even spend the children's future inheritance. After all, he'd not cared about spending their child support money on himself, instead of on their care.

Richard and I met with an estate-planning attorney who confirmed that Richard would have no parental rights if I passed away. I wrote a letter to the court, witnessed by our estate-planning attorney, which would be presented to the judge in the event that I died before the new court orders were signed. The letter provided a detailed time-line of Eugene's life and alcoholism along with my plea that, upon my death, he not be awarded custody until a hearing determined what was in the children's best interests.

It was obvious that Eugene had no intention of ever paying the past-due and future child support. This was proven later on when he told me, by phone, that, if we garnished his wages, he'd just "quit" his job. In a preliminary hearing, he tried to convince the court that we had a verbal agreement regarding child support (we did not). The court representative quickly silenced Eugene when he told him that even a signed and witnessed written agreement can't negate a court order (our divorce decree).

While Eugene was in Peru, I spoke to him by phone. Since he wasn't paying child support and couldn't take care of the children when he had visitation, and since he also wasn't able to care for them financially, and since he rarely called and didn't seem to want much to do with them anyway, perhaps it would be in everyone's best interests if he gave up his parental rights. He said he would think about it.

Months later, after he'd returned to the U.S., he finally told me he'd decided not to give up his parental rights. That was fine, provided he agreed to supervised visitation. At one point, he said, "I'll sign anything." I didn't believe him, of course.

The first legal step was to move jurisdiction of our case from Texas (where we'd gotten divorced) to Maine (where the children, Richard and I had lived for two years). That was accomplished easily because the children had resided in Maine for more than six months. That also meant I wouldn't have to fly to Texas for hearings.

Eugene initially threatened to fight me in Texas courts. However, he moved to Georgia soon after, so the jurisdiction change would have been easily obtained anyway. Just before he moved to Georgia, when he threatened to fight the court action, several abusive phone calls occurred. One night, he called and I went into our office so the children couldn't hear the conversation. I was listening to him threaten to get custody of the children and was getting quite distraught. I hung up on him. When I turned around, I found Mack, Alexandra, and Robert all standing silently behind me. They'd heard everything. I told them not to worry, that the judge would only do what was absolutely best for them, not what was best for Eugene.

Just before the holidays that year, Alexandra and Robert had been working on anger management with their therapists. They learned that it's okay to be mad at your parents and it's okay to not want to talk to somebody when you're mad at them. Sometimes, forcing a child to be polite hurts the child emotionally. Basically, nobody should force another person, especially a child, to talk to someone they're uncomfortable speaking to. So, on Christmas Day, when Eugene called, Alexandra and Robert refused to talk to him. Eugene accused me of not allowing them to speak to him. But, when we were talking, they were both sitting right there. I told him they were right there and both refused to take the phone.

Alexandra and Robert were visibly empowered by their decision. They were both learning that they could control their relationship with their father and were no longer bound, psychologically, by only his wants and needs. They had wants and needs of their own and had the power to choose their own actions and results.

These sporadic and tense phone battles continued and appeared to bring his Divorce Psychosis once more to a boil. It was like we were getting divorced all over again!

However, the miles between us and Eugene, and the fact that I had Richard here to protect and support us (physically and emotionally), made these episodes almost bearable. I had to hang up on Eugene many times when his phone calls became repeated and ridiculous. One phone call resulted in him accusing me of having an affair with his uncle. He also threatened to tell the children things about me that would only harm them psychologically, and he laughed about it!

These statements showed not only how desperate he was, but also how, after all these years, he still put his own selfish psychological needs ahead of the children's needs. While Eugene had a good laugh when making me uncomfortable, he never realized how his threats portrayed his ultimate goal to all involved, which was to hurt me emotionally. It was obvious to everyone, including the court, that Eugene was still putting himself first, and the children last.

While court orders appeared, were changed, and resubmitted, the phone calls slowed down. Once the police were finally able to serve Eugene with the new orders, he went ballistic. He was expecting papers on supervised visitation, but he was not expecting papers ordering him to pay past and current child support, along with a hefty chunk of interest. He said he could no longer trust me. Huh? I explained to him that I wasn't paying thousands to an attorney and not pursuing the child support he owed the children, too.

Months later, in mediation, he tried to weasel out of paying the past-due child support by lying and claiming that I owed him money for his credit card bills (which he claimed responsibility for in the divorce decree), and the sale of the house (which he took all profits from after blackmailing me), and that I stole or sold/gave away his woodworking tools (which he'd already admitted to picking up years ago). He made a few other ridiculous claims as well.

It quickly became obvious that he'd come to mediation armed with a list of fictitious debts that he claimed he planned to "sue" me for, all concocted to try to wrestle down the amount he owed in child support and medical expenses, which was more than $30,000. I felt like he and my attorney were negotiating the price of a used car instead of the future well being of three innocent children. It was one of the saddest things I've ever experienced.

At the end of mediation, he chose to give up his parental rights (give the children up for adoption) instead of paying any past or future child support. He was then ordered to appear before a judge in Georgia to relinquish his parental rights. I told my lawyer, "Just watch. He won't go until after the new year so he will be able to claim the children on his tax return one last time." Though the Georgia court clerk told my attorney they tried to get Eugene in earlier, he requested a later date. Eugene didn't go to court and sign the

> *My attorney was shaking her head and said, "He just sold his kids for $30,000." Pathetic, isn't it?*

papers until January 2nd. Coincidence? I don't think so.

After the mediation ended, the mediator stood up, shook her head, frowned and me, and muttered, "Wow."

My attorney was shaking her head as well and said, "He just sold his kids for $30,000."

Pathetic isn't it? I've met lots of men who were behind on child support, and even men who didn't think it was fair or that they had to pay too much. But I've never met a man who gave up his children to get out of paying it.

So, why did I allow him to do it? Since he called the children so seldom, and since he refused to pay child support, and since visiting him put them in danger, it was obvious that his top priority was not his children. And, why should the children be forced to visit someone who endangers their welfare, neglects them, and gives the impression that they're not wanted?

On February 19th of this year, Richard, Mack, Alexandra, Robert, Max (the new baby), and I all appeared in court. Richard was honored to be adopting Mack, Alexandra and Robert, and they were all excited about making it official, since they'd already considered him their daddy for four years.

During the entire adoption process, we approached the situation from a positive angle for the children's sakes. It was never "your father doesn't want you." It was, "Richard gets to pick who his children are, and he chooses you!" So, they know Richard chose them to be his, legally, because they're special and because he loves them so much.

Few men would accept the financial (and emotional) responsibility for three children that are not biologically theirs. Richard had to acknowledge to the court that he understood he would be responsible for child support for the children if we ever divorced. He readily agreed. He loves them that much!

Richard is, in every sense of the word, Mack, Alexandra and Robert's daddy. I will never be able to express to Richard, in words, the special gift he has given to my children...our children.

Many women who have been married and divorced more than once joke that they seem to keep marrying the same kind of man over and over again. I was lucky. My mother says I married the "polar opposite" of Eugene. And, she's right, I did.

If you were in an abusive relationship, remember the traits that were associated with your ex-husband's personality. Avoid those personality types when searching for your new mate.

There really are good, honorable men in this world. If you're patient and willing, you, like all the women in this book, will survive this nasty process of divorce. Don't give up! Your happiness is within reach! If you need some emotional support or advice, please send an email my way. I'm at: angela@angelahoy.com

Index

About the Author

Angela Hoy lives with her husband, Richard, and their children, Mack, Alexandra, Robert (not the children's real names) and Max on the beautiful Penobscot River in Bangor, Maine.

Angela and Richard are the owners of WritersWeekly.com and Booklocker.com. WritersWeekly.com is the FREE marketing emag for writers featuring new freelance job listings and paying markets every Wednesday. If you're a writer, or want to be a writer, subscribe today at: http://www.writersweekly.com

New subscribers receive the FREE ebook, How to Be a Freelance Writer (includes 103 paying markets!).

Booklocker.com, your bookstore for the unique, eclectic and different, publishes electronic and print on demand (POD) books for authors. Low setup fees, high royalties, monthly royalty payments, and authors keep all rights to their books. See: http://www.booklocker.com

Angela's Other Books:

· How to Be a Syndicated Newspaper Columnist (includes database of 6,000+ newspapers and 100+ syndicates)

· Profitable Email Publishing: How to Publish a Profitable Emag

· How to Write, Publish and Sell Ebooks

· How to Publish and Promote Online (co-written with M.J. Rose)

Angela's Publications:

· WritersWeekly.com – Free via email every Wednesday

· The Write Markets Report - $11.95/year. See: http://www.writersweekly.com/index-twmr.htm

Angela's Online Class:

· How to Remember, Write and Publish Your Life Story

For more details, see: http://www.angelahoy.com

FREE COPY OF THIS BOOK AVAILABLE ONLINE

This book is available as an electronic book (ebook) for free online to any woman who needs it. See: http://www.angelahoy.com

Printed in the United States
1440900002B/280-282